MAKING IT HAPPEN
The Harry Moseley Story

Georgina Moseley
With Simon Goodyear

Dedication

This book is dedicated to the short but inspirational life of Harry Moseley. My son, best friend and hero whom we lost tragically on 8th October 2011, aged just eleven years old.

Also, to Harry's Grandad, **Thomas Moseley** *(Tommy) who joined Harry very suddenly on 6th January 2012.*

And finally to Robert Harley, Harry's special friend and the inspiration for 'HelpHarryHelpOthers', who died 1st August 2009, also from brain cancer, four weeks after Harry started his campaign.

First published in Great Britain in 2012 by The Derby Books Publishing Company Limited, 3 The Parker Centre, Derby, DE21 4SZ.

Copyright © Simon Goodyear, 2012

ISBN 978-1-78091-052-9

Printed and bound by Gomer.

Contents

Foreword
By John Terry

John Terry is a professional footballer who plays in the centre-back position. He is the most successful captain in Chelsea Football Club's history and the former captain of the England national team.

I first met Harry when he was only ten years old. Frank Lampard (my Chelsea teammate) and I went to meet him at an England Footballers Foundation event and on the day we had to speak to the press and media. Both Frank and I were quite nervous about doing it, but young Harry got up and gave the most incredible, inspirational speech.

Harry was bright and intelligent and someone who cared very much about others. Although Harry was very ill himself, he really wanted to help others. His story really has broken my heart. He was such a strong character and he's done so much for other people, it was really an inspiration for us when we met him.

Foreword
By Ben Shephard

Ben Shephard is an English television presenter. He notably hosted ITV's flagship breakfast show GMTV for seven years, before leaving to join Sky Sports.

Harry was ten years old when I first met him and he had an inoperable brain tumour and yet at no point did that govern his life. His life was all about the time he had left and making a difference for other people who had brain cancer.

Harry was a shining example of what can happen if you give yourself a challenge. Nothing was too small for him; nothing was too big for him. Nobody was beyond his touch. He was the most incredible person I have ever met and I miss him every day.

A Note from the Author

Imust admit that, like many other people, I knew little about Harry Moseley until I saw his beaming little face light up on my TV local news. Not already being part of the Twitter community at the time, I quickly joined and checked out Harry's profile, which read (this is how Harry wrote it on his Twitter profile):

'I'm 11 and have an inoperable brain tumour.
I raise money for brain cancer research. Make bracelets & do public speaking. Helped to raise over £650,000.'

How could I not follow this brave and inspirational little boy?

Days later, on 8th October 2011, the world had lost Harry to the dreaded disease which had claimed the lives of my own mother and my father (who, coincidently, passed away on the same date as Harry, but in 2008). When I had heard of Harry's death I knew I wanted to do my bit to keep Harry's legacy alive.

I contacted Harry's brave and wonderful mum, Georgina (via Twitter) several weeks after Harry's death and told her of my idea of writing a book about Harry. Little did I know that it was one of Harry's dreams to have a book written about him, so when Georgina agreed for me to write it, I was excited and honoured at the prospect of fulfilling one of Harry's dreams, even though he would never see the final product.

It feels very special to be the author a book that a brave and selfless eleven-year-old boy inspired me to write. How cool and novel is that? It was a journey full of joy, excitement and the odd tear here and there, reliving the life of an amazing little boy, who has inspired millions of children and adults alike, across the globe.

Just as Harry intended, all my royalties from this book are being passed to Harry's charity so it can continue to help others like Harry would want.

I do hope you enjoy this book but be warned: tissues are essential.

Simon Goodyear
www.soccerbiographies.com

Prologue

An inspirational story of a real life angel

'My story began in 2007. I had problems with my eyes, so after lots of visits to the opticians and the local hospital, the doctors gave me an MRI scan. They told me that I have a brain tumour which can't be operated on as it's in a dangerous place, deep in my brain. I began chemotherapy, but it didn't work and my tumour grew. My only other option was radiotherapy.'
Harry Moseley, August 2011

The Harry Moseley Story – 'Making it Happen' – is a true account of how a 'normal' little boy with big dreams and a selfless, compassionate outlook on life proved that, with hard work, determination and a bit of cheek, anyone can achieve the goals they set themselves in life.

This is an emotional, heart-warming and truly inspirational account – told by Harry's mum and soul mate, Georgina – of how a little boy's dream of helping others changed the lives of millions and it will probably make you take a look at yourself in the process. Harry was diagnosed with brain cancer in 2007 at the age of seven. This book shows how, inspired by a friend who was also suffering from brain cancer, Harry evolved his simple ideas and philosophy into a global entrepreneurial campaign using all the social media tools available to him, including his beloved Twitter. The book emphasises that we can all achieve anything in life and 'make it happen' if we believe in ourselves, as long as we are committed to our goals and are passionate about our dreams.

Harry gripped the nation by making and selling beaded bracelets all by himself, with the proceeds he raised going to charity. He also organised and arranged to meet CEOs of large organisations and did presentations at school assemblies and at large public events in front of the local and national media, talking about his business ideas. All this was achieved by Harry himself in the face of adversity and fighting a dreadful disease. With this kind of determination, nothing was unachievable for young Harry. During his fight against brain cancer, Harry befriended many people via his Twitter account, including adults and children, younger and older than himself, from all sorts of backgrounds. He also captured the hearts and minds of many famous celebrities and sports stars including Chris Evans, Duncan Bannatyne, John Terry, Gary Lineker, Wincey Willis, Ian Taylor and Ben Shephard, to name but a few.

When Harry sadly passed away in October 2011, he had raised a staggering £650,000 for his chosen charities and this has now risen to over £1.1 million at the time of writing. Harry won many high profile awards while he was alive and since his death many more achievements have been awarded in his name. His legacy lives on and his dreams are now starting to become reality, thanks to his mum and his army of followers who continue to kindly organise events in his memory, all 'making it happen' for Harry.

1

The World According to Harry

'If I look OK and feel OK, then I am OK.'
Harry Moseley

Harry was born on the 22nd February 2000 at Heartlands Hospital in East Birmingham. Having already given birth to a boy and a girl I was convinced all along that I was going to be having another baby girl; I don't know why but I had a gut feeling about it. Call it a mother's instinct or something, but I was that adamant about the sex of my child that the name had already been chosen. She was going to be called 'Courtney'. Then at 7.30pm on that cold February evening, I was proven so wrong. Right from the very moment Harry made his entrance into the world there was no mistaking he was a boy, because as soon as the nurse had placed Harry into my arms, he peed all over me and we just saw this fountain of water and I thought: 'Here we go.' That really showed us Harry's character, right from the first minutes of his life!

We have always been a very close-knit family with the old-fashioned family values of togetherness being so important to us. We didn't go out socialising with our friends very much, as we nearly always went out as a family. We had the children before we got married and didn't have a honeymoon as such, even though we had offers from the family to look after the children which we always refused because we wanted them to be fully involved in our lives, right from the start. It wasn't just about me and Harry's dad, Darren – it was always about the five of us as a family unit. Even for special occasions like Valentine's Day, Mother's Day and Father's Day, we would go out as a family, with the children in tow. Our lives have always been like that from day one.

I was twenty-five years old when I had Harry. Although I'd had my first child, Danielle, when I was quite young, I'd always worked hard (like most mothers) and was very career-minded and wanted the best for my family so I could give Dani, Louie and Harry the best things in life. I'd always worked in sales and I was a Sales Manager when I had Harry. I certainly wasn't what you would call clever, but that made me more determined to work incredibly hard for the sake of my family and I wanted to succeed as best I could in my chosen field. In our mid-twenties, Darren and I were so content and life seemed to be coming together for us quite nicely. Darren and I knew our family was complete with the addition of Harry and we were just so tight as a family unit, like a jigsaw puzzle. Harry was that final missing piece which seemed to just slot into place.

Right from a young age Harry loved his paddling pool. He would sit in it as soon as the sun came out and would stay in there all day long, if he could. We'd have hours and hours of fun just with a paddling pool full of water. People always say it's the simple things that give the most pleasure to children, and that was certainly the case with Harry. Children love to improvise and Harry was no different to anyone else. Whereas other children would dip in and out of their paddling pool because of the temperature of the water, Harry didn't care how cold it was and would sit in it just playing with his little action figures, talking to himself as children do when they play on their own. Those memories will always be among my fondest of Harry.

Harry was always such a happy, contented baby and seemed to smile all the time – huge smiles and the biggest, brightest blue eyes you'd ever seen. Growing up, he was always such a healthy little boy and there were never any signs of illness at all. Harry was what you would describe as your 'average toddler', really. He had a good sense of humour and was very funny to listen to as a child. As soon as he'd found his feet, he would love to run around the house and always posed for a photograph when the camera was out. He would think nothing of running round with no clothes on, maybe donning one of his sister's hats or something ridiculous and always wore a big cheesy grin on his face, as if he'd been up to no good. I'm sure he would have gone out of the house like it if we had allowed him to! He loved to get up and sing at family parties or when we were on holiday and sometimes with no music to sing along to. Harry was just a genuine joy to be with.

The bond between the two boys was something special. Harry always looked up to Louie and thought of him as his 'hero' and they developed such a special friendship together right from an early age. Harry couldn't pronounce his brother's name correctly, though, and it usually came out something like 'Yooey', which always amused us. The two boys never seemed to be apart for very long and even shared a bedroom together, which encouraged the special bond they had. Whatever Louie was doing or whatever he had, Harry was always interested in it, as Harry was very inquisitive. It was really nice to watch, because Harry was very much like his elder brother in terms of build and stature, but quite the opposite in many other ways. Harry and Louie had very different personalities, but it was like they had some sort of balance between them; Harry had this 'cheeky chappy' persona – an outgoing and quite confident character who wasn't very sporty at all – whereas Louie was the opposite in a lot of ways, but that's what made them tick, I guess. Harry was also really close with his big sister and was really affectionate with her from a young age. Harry was always an affectionate, loving boy and would always give her hugs and kisses. He would always go into her room and chat to her on her bed. He loved it when her girlfriends came, too, and he always wanted to be involved in their girlie conversations.

Harry was such a beautiful person, with the fun and charm to brighten up any room he entered. This was a great gift for such a young lad and one not many adults can boast, let alone children. For someone so young, he had it all: charm, wit, love, fun, cheek, humour and he had the compassion and selflessness which, all added together, made him the person he was.

Harry was also so confident as a young boy and I remember one summer holiday where Harry had spent the entire day in the pool. During the evening we were at a family bar. There was a singer on stage and she decided to ask if anyone would like to get up on stage to sing. Harry's hand shot straight up and he wanted to sing his favourite song, which, at the time, was Father and Son by Boyzone (the original was by Cat Stevens). This was pretty unusual for a young lad because it's quite a sad song. The band didn't have the music but Harry, who was just six years old, didn't mind and said confidently: 'That's alright. I'll sing it without music.' Being the way he was, Harry got up and sang his little heart out in front of quite a large audience.

During his nursery and infants days, although Harry blended in like any other kid, he was very, very confident for someone so young and he was very intelligent, too. He would always get excited to receive stickers from the teachers for being good at different subjects and couldn't wait to show us his books when he got home, as well. However, it was during the spring of 2006 that we started to notice the way Harry was looking at his books at home. He wasn't looking at them in the normal way or the way he had learned to. Although he had the book directly in front of him, his head was tilted to one side at a ninety degree angle, but the strange thing was he was still reading the words in the book all the same. I thought it was rather unusual, so I said to him: 'Harry, are you doing that on purpose?' He obviously didn't think anything was untoward, so I then observed him for an hour or so. Then he went to put the TV on after he had finished his reading and again, even though the TV was right in front of him, his head was at an angle but he was looking straight at the screen. Even though it was quite late in the afternoon by this time, I rang a very small Opticians practice in the local area, rather than one of the large group practices, and they actually opened up for us because we were quite worried about the situation. I thought it might be nothing, but as a mother you can't take any chances when it comes to your child's health. It didn't even enter our heads that there could be anything seriously wrong with Harry. We just thought there was something wrong with his eyes or maybe he was just tired. Initially, we thought he may need glasses to correct his vision or a patch maybe, to strengthen one of his eyes. When the optician examined him, he said he could see something like a shadow at the back of Harry's eyes, and he immediately referred him to Heartlands Hospital. I went straight into panic mode as any mother probably would, but we couldn't do anything until the hospital appointment arrived and then we would hopefully know more about Harry's condition. Bearing in mind Harry had always been a healthy little boy, this news came as a complete shock to us.

When the appointment with the eye consultant finally arrived, around early June, they firstly tested his eyesight by placing a patch over one of his eyes. This proved that his left eye wasn't as good, so the consultant then put the patch over Harry's right eye which he then had to wear all day, every day in order to strengthen up his left eye. These appointments continued every four weeks right up until the September and every time we went back for a check-up, the tests proved his eyesight had deteriorated somewhat from the previous appointment. By this time, we were getting very concerned, and then one of the consultants called us into the office and said that although they were aware Harry's eyesight was deteriorating, they didn't know what was going on and suggested he should continue to be monitored. I wasn't happy with this as it had dragged on for quite some time with no diagnosis, so I disagreed with the consultant's suggestion. I stated that for Harry's eyesight to deteriorate every four weeks, there must be something causing it and the consultant finally agreed and then decided to refer Harry for a MRI scan, mainly to put our minds at rest. We would hopefully know what was causing his eyesight to weaken and that at least gave me some comfort. I couldn't understand why the consultant had taken so much time over making a decision to refer Harry to Heartlands Hospital to have an MRI scan, but I'm not an optician or a doctor, so I had no choice but to go along with whatever they decided was best for Harry. In the meantime, whilst Harry was waiting for the MRI scan, he still went to the hospital for further eye tests.

Christmas had come and gone and we still hadn't heard from the hospital about the appointment for the MRI scan and this continued well into the New Year until the appointment date come through for 14th February – Valentine's Day. I was disgusted at the amount of time it had taken the NHS to send us the appointment for a scan – more than five months! All this time had passed by and Harry's eyesight was getting progressively worse. We were not happy, to say the least, but now his appointment had arrived we thought we could finally get a diagnosis and hopefully some treatment for Harry.

Harry was chirpy on the morning of the scan, but he had to be put under a general anaesthetic, which he didn't like very much. When the scan was over, they took Harry back onto the ward and he gradually came round from the anaesthetic. The doctors followed shortly after, but I noticed that their general demeanour was different and the tone of their voices had completely changed. I kept saying to Darren that there had to be something wrong. Harry had been scanned for forty-five minutes – he was only meant to have been there for fifteen minutes – and that immediately told me something wasn't right. The doctor kept asking us questions about Harry's learning ability and if he had had any bangs on his head recently. I thought: 'What child doesn't bang their head from time to time? ' All I wanted to know was if there was anything wrong with my baby. Unfortunately, Harry's consultant wasn't on duty that day, so they asked us if we would come back the following day to see her. We refused because I wanted to see her there and then and I said I would drive to wherever she was to speak to her that day because I wanted answers to questions like: 'What's wrong with Harry?' They wouldn't tell me where she was, so we had to go home and suffer another night without knowing anything. I was so angry. That day must have been the longest day in our lives and overnight, we were thinking all sorts of things about Harry. What was wrong with him? Was he going to go blind? Little did we know then that this was the start of a lot of long and hard days ahead, not only for Harry but for the whole Moseley family.

When we went to the hospital for the appointment with Harry's consultant the next day, we had Harry with us and the consultant started examining his eyes again. It was at this point that she just let it out that the scan results had shown a 'mass' in Harry's brain. We didn't really comprehend what she was saying because it had come as a complete surprise and we weren't too sure what she was actually implying was wrong with Harry. 'A 'mass'? What does that mean?' The consultant tried to explain in simple terms what the diagnosis was and said that Harry would need surgery to remove the 'mass'. We were also told that the 'mass' was a tumour, but they didn't know at that stage if it was cancerous. We were hopeful that he could be cured by the operation, but then the consultant looked rather negative and said they had sent all of the details by taxi to the Birmingham Children's Hospital for one of the neurosurgeons to offer a second opinion. They said they would make contact with us once he had established how to tackle the tumour. We were asked to go home and sit and wait for a phone call, which would hopefully provide us with more information. We knew very little at that stage, except that Harry had a tumour on the brain. On our way home from the hospital, Harry was in the back of the car, quiet and subdued, which wasn't normal for him, as he usually burst out into song every time he was in the car. On this occasion, he was obviously holding in his emotions, knowing that there was something wrong with him. For the whole journey home I don't remember anyone speaking. It was a horrible atmosphere and a horrible journey and it had been a dreadful day! Darren and I were trying our hardest to hold in our emotions for Harry's sake, but we were both so numb and I felt like I just wanted to cry. We were both wondering what this all meant for Harry.

My initial instinct was to 'Google' everything there was to know about the words 'brain tumour' and 'mass' but I just couldn't, through fear of upsetting myself, so I decided to wait until I heard it directly from the doctors. Somehow, we had to break the bad news to the children and the rest of our family, even though we had received just the bare bones of information from the consultant. When Louie and Danielle arrived home from school that day, we had to find the right time and the right words to tell them the news about Harry. We eventually plucked up enough courage and we just said that Harry had a 'lump' in his brain which shouldn't be there. It would probably mean Harry would have to be given something to make him sleep, in order to have an operation. We had to break the information down into 'kiddie' terms so as not to overcomplicate things for them and not to worry them too much. Some of our parents probably grasped the significance of the news more than we did, as we were still in a state of shock and couldn't comprehend what we had been told by the consultant. Harry seemed fine with that bit of information and, as parents, we just wanted to keep everything as 'normal' and routine as we always had done. The truth was that, inside, we were terrified for our son.

Another twenty-four hours had passed by and I got even more impatient that we had not received any more detailed information from the consultant, so I phoned the Birmingham Children's Hospital repeatedly, to try and find out any further information. I wanted to know all about the tumour. Would they have to operate on Harry? Was Harry

OK? Was Harry's sight in jeopardy? Was Harry's life threatened by this tumour? There were so many questions going round in my head, I couldn't think straight. We were all in a state of complete panic and it was the not knowing which we hated more than anything else. Everything started to run through my head; good things as well as bad thoughts. I was thinking the most stupid and trivial things like: would Harry be able to sit in his paddling pool or play football with Louie again? During this period we were conscious not to show Harry our true feelings and what was happening 'behind the scenes'. Harry was only six years old and it was only a week before his seventh birthday and we didn't know what was really going on. We didn't understand what a 'tumour' was and what it meant to his future, but Harry knew enough to grasp the simple fact that he had something wrong with him.

The next few weeks were torture, waiting for the next appointment with the neurosurgeon at the Children's Hospital. But in the meantime, we had to carry on normally as a family. The children (including Harry) continued going to school and the teachers were advised of the situation. We asked them to contact us if the slightest thing happened with Harry; if he started being sick or he complained of having a headache. Darren and I both carried on going to work but, for me, it was really hard to concentrate on anything other than Harry, trying to grasp what it all meant and not knowing what the future would hold. We both struggled through those few weeks waiting for the next appointment to arrive, when we would hopefully learn a bit more.

The day finally came when we would see the neurosurgeon at Birmingham Children's Hospital, which has one of the finest neurology units in the country, so in that respect we knew Harry would be in good hands. We were full of anticipation that we were hopefully going to hear some more news; some better news. Whatever the outcome we would face it head on as a family unit, but we just wanted to hear a definitive answer from the consultant. However, there was a horrible aura about the room we were led into and the consultant seemed very cold in the way he delivered the news to us. It was all very bizarre. The surgeon sat us down and said: 'I want Harry to have another MRI scan.' Darren and I just looked at each other. We were bemused. 'Why? He's had one already,' I replied. The neurosurgeon who spoke to us was admittedly fantastic at his job, but his people skills were pretty poor. He may have been good at the technical side of being a surgeon but when it came to actually explaining to us what was wrong with Harry and what the consequences were, his communication skills left a lot to be desired. The surgeon explained to us in his own way that he needed to see where the tumour stemmed from and what type of brain tumour it was before anything else. I just thought a brain tumour was a brain tumour. Little did I know at the time that there were many different types of brain tumour and so many locations they could start from. They needed to determine the route of the tumour, where it started and where it was going and unfortunately the previous scan didn't show that. He also explained that Harry's tumour was quite large for his age and it was pushing on a lot of things inside the brain and he needed to find out where the stem of it was. We were hoping that Harry would be able to have the scan on that day, but we were told that we would have to wait for yet another appointment. There was no more to be said and we walked out of that room not really knowing anything new. We had waited weeks and weeks for the appointment in the first place and had endured many sleepless nights thinking about what the surgeon might say, but we were still none the wiser and had been told to wait even longer. However, we kept positive, thinking that Harry would have the surgery soon and within six or twelve months it would all be over and he would be well again.

As a family, we always had the philosophy of not worrying about something until you know what you're faced with and just trying to carry on as normal, because you may end up worrying about nothing at all. That's exactly what we did, although again, it was hard to focus on anything else. A few weeks passed by and we eventually got the app-ointment for the second scan which was followed, several days later, by a biopsy. While Harry was in hospital for the biopsy (which was bad enough, as he had to have a tiny instrument inserted through his brain to reach the tumour in order to extract particles of it for testing in the laboratories) we met another consultant called Dr Peet for the first time. Dr Peet was an oncologist and a really lovely man indeed. He was like a breath of fresh air as he seemed so friendly, compassionate and very much a 'people person'. Harry just seemed to click with him straight away. I explained to him about all the waiting we'd had to endure and you could see in his eyes that he genuinely 'felt' for us. He explained to us that, depending on the results of the biopsy, he might be the person who would look after Harry. I begged him to call us as soon as he received any news about the biopsy so we could find out immediately what Harry's fate would be. No more than an hour after arriving home with Harry from the hospital after his ordeal, Dr Peet rang to say he had received some news. It was late on a Friday afternoon but I pleaded for us to see him immediately and he agreed. Darren and I phoned for a taxi and headed back to the oncology clinic at the hospital. Until I had been there in the morning, I'd never heard the word 'oncology' before, but it had now become all too familiar. We arrived back at the clinic to find it was deserted, being late on a Friday afternoon, but all around the waiting room was information about cancer and I started to get really nervous. We were shown into Dr Peet's office and he explained that Harry's tumour was inoperable, due to its location. He explained it was too dangerous to operate because it was located in the middle of Harry's brain and there was no way to access it. Our thoughts immediately turned to Harry and to the fact that he wouldn't have to go through the terrible ordeal of having surgery. At the same time, any thoughts that after six months our lives would be back to normal were well and truly over. I felt sick inside and just wanted to understand every single word Dr Peet was telling us. Radiotherapy was also ruled out at this stage because of Harry's age and the side-effects it would have on the good parts of the brain for someone so young. Then all I heard was the words '...the only option for Harry is chemotherapy.' When I thought of the word 'chemotherapy' I immediately thought of cancer and Dr Peet explained all about Harry's tumour being a 'low grade glioma' – a slow-growing cancer – though he couldn't explain why it was there. It may have been there from birth and it was quite big, measuring around 5cm in diameter. However, it gave us a little hope as it was 'slow-growing' and at this point we were desperate to cling on to something. Then he went on to explain that there was a possibility it would be harder and slower to shrink the tumour. Fast-growing cancers react better to drugs and, if the treatment works, they tend to respond more quickly. We were told Harry had to have eighteen months of chemotherapy, which involved him having to have three types of chemo intravenously through a central line, which was to be inserted into his chest. Harry was to attend hospital three days a week for the first three months, because they wanted to start intensive chemo. Dr Peet told us about all the side-effects and warned us that it might frequently make Harry quite poorly. He also said that, besides the three days per week having chemo, Harry might end up staying in hospital if he got a temperature. Having chemo weakens the immune system, making it harder for the body to fight off colds and infections. Therefore, even if Harry had a slight temperature or if he was not well in himself we would have to rush him straight to hospital to have a few days on antibiotics through a drip. At this point, we had no idea of (and nor did we even think about) the impact this would have on our family, its routine or our lifestyle. All we could think about was Harry. Why Harry?

Dr Peet was wonderful and the way he spoke to us was first class. He described the situation in simple terms and didn't blind us with science. He answered every question we put to him until he realised we had taken in as much information as we could and it was time for us to go home to digest it all. He wanted us to go away and think about it over that weekend and asked us to come back to see him on the following Tuesday in his clinic that he held every week.

It was only when we had got home after that meeting that we actually took in what he had told us and the seriousness of the situation. For the second time in the space of a few weeks, we had to sit the children down to tell them some dreadful news about their brother, but this time we had all the facts to hand. Any parent who has tried to explain a difficult situation to children at such tender ages would agree that it has to be one of the hardest things in the world to do. All I thought about was the impact it would have on our family for the next eighteen months until the chemotherapy treatment had been completed and, hopefully, Harry would be cured. That was our dearest wish and we lived in hope, every single day. I knew that, from then on, our family life and our routine as we knew it would change for ever, but it was something we had to accept and live with, if we were to support Harry. Darren and I were heading into the unknown and we feared not only for Harry but for our entire family and how this would affect them. At the same time, we had to be strong for the children and, while Harry had just been diagnosed with a serious life threatening illness, we all had to just take whatever was thrown at us, just like every other family going through the same situation has to. For Harry's sake, we also had to remain positive and ensure that we were there for all the children every step of the way. As painful as it was, all we could do was get on with it.

It's hard enough explaining these situations to adults, but talking things through with your own children is even harder, as we had to explain everything in small chunks and in the simplest terms so as not to overload them with facts and not make them more upset than they already were. Harry's brother Louie was only ten years old at the time and his sister Dani was thirteen. We trod very carefully by saying things like: 'Harry's lump in his brain is called a brain tumour and it's a type of cancer. It's something that shouldn't be there and the doctors don't know why it is there. It could have been there from birth but they just don't know.' I could see the blankness in their expression on their tiny faces. They had no real understanding of what this all meant and why should they have? They were just children. I went on: '...because Harry's lump is right in the centre of his brain, the doctors can't get to it by doing an operation and so Harry has to have some really strong medicine called chemotherapy. He has to go to hospital and a 'wiggly line' has to be put into Harry's chest so that when he visits hospital three days a week to have chemo, they can give it him through the 'wiggly line' so the 'magic medicine' can get to all the parts of his body and, in time, it will make the tumour shrink. The 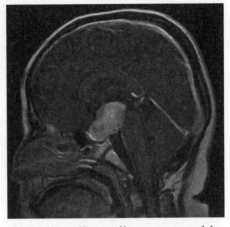 chemo may make Harry feel quite tired as it's really, really strong and he may lose his hair.' Harry, being Harry, just lightened the air by saying: 'Can I have a beanie hat then, mum?'

I explained to the children that we had to go through a bit of a change in routine while Harry underwent his treatment but after his treatment of eighteen months (or that's what we thought at the time) Harry would hopefully be cured and things would be back to normal. I remember Dani crying, as she was a few years older and, in her own way, I think she understood it more than Louie did and she knew how ill Harry was. Harry was still being himself – laughing and joking and remaining positive – but his brother was just so quiet and withdrawn. I felt for them all. It was just too much for any child to take in and, even for us, it was so hard to understand, as Harry didn't look ill in any way and didn't have any symptoms of being ill. In fact, he looked a picture of health and was the same 'cheeky chappy' he had always been. I told them all they could ask me anything they wanted whenever they wanted to and that they could also come to the hospital if they chose to, so they could try to understand more by seeing how the chemo was administered and the side-effects it had on Harry. I left it open for them. I wanted them to be as involved as they wanted to be. The choice was entirely theirs.

Fortunately, we wouldn't have to wait too long for the first round of chemo to begin, but before that, poor Harry had to have a line put in his chest, which was a trauma in itself for a seven-year-old. Harry thought it was kind of 'cool', though, to have this tube (which we called a 'wiggly') sticking out of his chest. The 'wiggly' led into a small bag and he would have to carry it around with him twenty-four hours a day. Harry's cancer journey was about to commence with the chemotherapy and we would be with him all the way.

Chemotherapy is a type of treatment for cancer using a combination of drugs. The most common chemotherapy agents act by killing cells that divide rapidly, one of the main properties of most cancer cells. This means that chemotherapy also harms cells that divide rapidly under normal circumstances: cells in the bone marrow, digestive tract, and hair follicles. This results in the most common side-effects which include decreased production of blood cells, the inflammation of the lining of the digestive tract and alopecia (hair loss). The treatment involved going to the Children's Hospital in Birmingham three days a week to administer the chemo through a drip, which would go into Harry's 'wiggly' in his chest. As I've mentioned, we were warned that the chemo would make Harry really poorly and that he might end up spending more than the three days in hospital at a time if he complained of even the slightest little thing like having a temperature or a headache. Initially, when we were told that we would have to take Harry there three days a week, we thought about how we would cope, what with looking after the other children, our own lives, and our daily routine, as well as having to go to work. Oh, and trying to get some sleep in between. Obviously, being Harry's mum, I had to be with him every time we went to the hospital. It meant a major change to our lives and we had only just realised what sort of an impact it had on us as a family. When we sat in front of the doctors at the Children's Hospital and they tried to explain Harry's treatment to all of us, things like our day-to-day routine didn't even occur to us, because we just focused on the news they were giving us at the time and we didn't even think about any impacts on our lives.

Harry's treatment started shortly after hearing the news from Dr Peet and after a few days we soon settled into some sort of a new routine – we had to, because we didn't have time to think about anything else, as everything was now happening so quickly. Once one session was over, it seemed like the next wasn't too far away and then the routine started all over again. It seemed like each session took up the whole day. Yet for Harry, it was kind of fun and he just smiled his way through it. They say children are tolerant of most things and Harry was very positive about it all, which was very brave for a seven-year-old boy. He seemed to understand just about everything he'd been told by the doctors, but the one thing he didn't grasp was that before the chemo started, he'd felt good, but the treatment (which would hopefully make him better) would make him feel sick at first. I don't know if Harry knew that he also had to have drugs to stop the sickness caused by the chemo. It all seemed a bit confusing for him, which was understandable.

After a few weeks, Harry was beginning to feel rough, tired and weak through all the chemo he had to have, but only on one occasion did he get upset. He cried and he said to me: 'Mum, I don't know what's wrong with me, but I don't feel like myself anymore.' That was the only time Harry ever commented on his situation and, to me, that said a lot about him as a person. Harry knew he had to have the treatment so he could stand a chance to get better and he had decided early on he just had to get on with it. He even learned every name of his chemo drugs off by heart – Vincristine, Etoposide and Carboplatin, which were the three different types of chemo he was having. He knew the name of the brain tumour he had – Pilocytic Astrocytoma. We all thought: 'Wow, Harry. How did you learn those names?' He had a laugh with his doctor and the nurses about which drug they were going to give him first. Harry loved all of that and wanted to learn those names and make light of his situation, which, however you look at it, was not a good one. That was the kind of spirit Harry had all the time. 'OK, I've got this tumour. What is it? What are the medicines you're giving me?' I guess you'd call it a kid's curiosity but Harry had an unusually inquisitive mind. As parents we were heartbroken, but Harry showed us the way to go and we had to follow in the same vein.

Three months into chemo in June 2007.

All we could do was to be there for him and love him through the situation. By this time he was so tired he had to be carried around in a wheelchair and I honestly thought we were going to lose Harry. We had already kind of expected that, because he was so weak and, visually, he'd started to look so, so seriously ill. It was the side-effects of the chemo that were taking their toll on him.

Harry actually liked his doctor, Andrew Peet, very much and got on with him really well. So much so that he called him his 'God'. Dr Peet not only had the medical knowledge but, in our eyes, he had the 'full package' – he was a person that every young doctor should aspire to be like. Dr Peet was (and still is) an oncologist consultant at Birmingham Children's Hospital and researcher at the University of Birmingham. His time was split between treating children like Harry who have brain tumours and researching better ways to diagnose and monitor these cancers. The hope is that his research will eventually lead to more tailored treatment for children with cancer, helping to save even more lives. Harry was fortunate to have such an experienced and influential doctor looking after him.

Harry was supposed to have eighteen months of chemo, but after only four months his treatment stopped because his young body was so weak and full of toxins and he just couldn't take any more of it. He had a month's break from it, so his body could recover and, soon after the break, Harry had to have another routine MRI scan. It was from the results of that scan that we learned that the treatment hadn't worked and the tumour had grown. Our hearts sank when the news was delivered by Dr Peet and alarm bells started to ring. I immediately thought that if the chemo hadn't worked and surgery wasn't an option, what could the doctors do now for Harry? They just had to do something. I felt sick and was shocked that the chemo hadn't done its job. It was the worst feeling in the world, knowing that his little body had been through so much because of the side-effects of the chemo and yet we were no further forward. I wanted to believe that they had got it all wrong and so I quizzed the doctors: 'Are you sure it has grown?' However, after seeing the results of the scan for ourselves we could see the growth all too clearly. I can't describe the emotions that poured through my body at that time, but I knew I had to keep calm and remain strong, because Harry was sat right next to us in the doctor's office. It was just so hard to take in, but we had to act as normally as we could for his sake, while at the same time I was crumbling inside, full of despair and the feeling of being so helpless. I even wished it was me instead of our little boy.

Why did it have to be our baby boy?

We had another meeting with the doctors the next day and they still ruled out surgery but said that they would consider radiotherapy as an alternative. However, we had to wait for about five or six weeks before Harry could begin the radiotherapy treatment and, for this period of time, Harry had to take steroids daily so that his tumour wouldn't get any bigger. Harry was allowed to remain at home during the time before the radiotherapy and as each day passed he started to recover from the effects of chemo. He began to put on weight, regained his strength and his hair was beginning to grow back as well. We couldn't comprehend that he was still so poorly, as he continued going to school and just living life to the full, like every average seven-year-old.

On 5th November 2007, Harry started his radiotherapy. This time we had to go to the Queen Elizabeth II Hospital in Birmingham five days a week for a period of six weeks. Radiotherapy is commonly applied to the cancerous tumour because of its ability to control cell growth. It's directed to a localised area of the body affected by the cancer. In Harry's case, it would have to be directed accurately to where the tumour was in the brain. Before the first couple of sessions, the doctors had to make a mask of Harry's head and a cold rubber jelly was put over his face, front and back, with small slits where his nose, mouth and eyes were. For a seven-year-old, it must have been a pretty frightening experience indeed. He had to lie on the bed, totally still, while this jelly set hard. We were told that the mask was required as a guide to where they had to aim the lasers for the radiotherapy and they had to be dead on: the lasers had to hit the tumour with pin-point accuracy.

Yet again, our routine had to change to accommodate the treatment, because every day we would have an ambulance come and pick us up to take us to the hospital and also it was coming up to the busy Christmas period, with the build-up starting to get into full swing. Harry, being Harry, made light of his situation again and decided to dress up in his Santa hat. He would also sing random Christmas songs and tell the odd joke or two to the ambulance driver and the other passengers en route to the hospital, just to lighten the mood. He was being his usual, cheery self. He just couldn't feel down about his situation so he thought he would use the time travelling to and from the hospital by making people laugh and trying to forget the horrid treatment he was about to receive.

Fortunately, each round of treatment was followed by a break at the weekend and we just had to wait and watch for any signs of Harry getting any worse. Throughout all of his treatment, Harry carried on going to school when he could and when he had the strength to. There was only one period when he was going through his treatment that he had to have a home tutor in because he wasn't well enough to go to school. Maybe he wasn't well enough or in the right frame of mind to go to school but more often than not he made the effort to attend. He just wanted to learn. There was the odd day here or there when we would get a phone call saying 'Harry's got a headache' and the school asked me to come and collect him. He loved being at school and being around his friends and hated being on his own at home. I think he probably taught some of his peers a lot of things about cancer and about the side-effects of the treatment. During the radiotherapy he lost a lot of his hair and had a red circle on top of his head caused by the radiation, together with two big bald patches at the side of his head. We felt for Harry in case he got bullied or picked on at school because of the way he looked. Children can be cruel sometimes and don't always understand what someone is going through. We couldn't shave his remaining hair off because the radiotherapy had burned his scalp and his head was very sensitive, but Harry didn't care what he looked like and just carried on regardless. When his hair began to fall out he would even make a joke of it by saying it was 'a magic trick'. Harry was obsessed with magic and he loved the fact that he could pull out a clump of his hair and make a joke of it.

Once Harry had completed the course of radiotherapy he continued to put on weight again very quickly. Part of the problem was the location of his tumour – right in the centre of the brain, probably the worst place for a tumour to be. Harry was taking a number of steroids to prevent swelling in his brain and this treatment lasted for about twelve weeks, but the side-effect of these steroids was that they caused bloating and weight gain. I don't know how he coped with it all, with the tumour and his weight gain, but he did extremely well. With the weight problem came the taunting at school as some of his school mates didn't understand what was wrong with Harry. All they saw was that Harry had stopped growing and had put on some weight and they thought he had eaten loads of food, but it obviously wasn't like that.

Even though Harry was a normal little boy he didn't eat excessively; he didn't eat sweets and chocolate like his brother did. We used to encourage Harry to ignore the comments and said to him: 'You know, Harry. This is not you being greedy. It's all beyond your control, a bit like your lump.' We used to call his tumour 'The Lump', to make it sound a bit friendlier. Deep down, Harry couldn't stand being the size he was and wanted to go to Weight Watchers because he was frustrated that his brother had a perfect-shaped body and was the one who ate chocolate, sweets and crisps, just like most other children do in their early teens. The cancer didn't bother Harry, but the impact of his weight gain did. Even his endocrine consultant (endocrine problems being the cause of hormone disorders) could feel the pain Harry was suffering caused by the growth and weight problems and, as time passed, it became more apparent. I tried my hardest to get him to forget the ignorance of some mindless people and said to him that they or their comments didn't matter, but he couldn't ignore it. I remember one day we were in Birmingham city centre following a hospital appointment. Harry, my mother and I were in a department store and while I was looking at something, I saw Harry in the next aisle and I could see him looking at some children's clothes, as he loved clothes, just like his brother did. Suddenly, he came up to me and appeared to be really upset about something, so I gave him a big hug and a kiss, held him tight to console him and said to him: 'Whatever's the matter, H?' He replied: 'Those two men were taking the 'mickey' out of my size.' I asked him to point them out to me. Once I'd calmed him down and had a conversation about how mindless and selfish some people could be, I asked my mother to take Harry out of the store, as I didn't want him to get upset again. At this point I was outraged and followed the two men to a busy area of the shop, where I confronted them at the top of my voice. If you can imagine the scene, I was in the middle of a busy city centre department store and I was furious because my son had been harassed about his size and found it in me from somewhere to confront two grown men face-to-face. I have no idea where it came from, as usually I'm so patient and calm in those situations. I'm so laid back and hate confrontation, but I was furious and I made sure the whole store knew what the two culprits had said to Harry and then told them about why Harry was a bigger than average lad. I saw their faces turn bright red and I asked them: 'Feel ashamed and embarrassed, do you? Good, because that's how you've made my little boy who's fighting cancer feel. I hope before you make a judgement about anyone ever again, you'll think before you open your mouths.' On that note I walked out of the store as though nothing had happened. With all that Harry was going through and with him getting on with it so positively and so amazingly, I wasn't about to let two mindless idiots bring him down.

To me, Harry was like a grown man in a little boy's body in many ways. He loved his Sunday roast. He loved vegetables, and green beans were his absolute favourite. Even when the doctor at the hospital asked him to choose his dinner, Harry brushed aside the pizzas, chicken nuggets, chips and smiley faces in place of a plate of vegetables with potatoes and meat;

the kind of stuff which wouldn't appeal to most other children, but that Harry loved. It was quite hard for him to take it all in and Harry couldn't understand why he had put on this weight because it wasn't through the type of food he was consuming. Harry kept thinking about the time he was like his brother, Louie, because he always looked up to his older brother but, for Harry, this was out of his control.

The one thing Harry did have control over was realising from an early age, soon after he was diagnosed, what he could do and what he couldn't do. He was very mature in the way he dealt with his illness; he didn't focus on what his illness meant he wasn't able to do or how it made him feel, but he focused on the positives – 'Well, what can I do? How can I change this and make things better and be happy?' In any person, especially someone so young, that's an amazing quality to have. He just got on with it and enjoyed the things he had control over, the things he could do and especially the things he could do well. Understandably, some people who are diagnosed with a terrible illness worry and focus on the negatives and what the illness does to them, rather than taking the opposite view – 'I can do this, even though I can't do that'. This kind of attitude was what made Harry such a special boy. We always encouraged him to follow his dreams and to do different things, but we also had to impose an element of control over his life, because of his situation and his age. We could never allow Harry to go away with friends or even entertain the thought of Harry going on a 'sleepover' at a friend's house or even going to birthday parties. Maybe some mothers were reluctant to invite Harry over because of his illness, too, which was completely understandable. As he was getting older and more independent, this was all becoming really hard for Harry to grasp. Some of his friends had started walking to school alone and were allowed to play out, away from home. I couldn't allow any of that for Harry, even if I did think he was old enough.

Following his radiotherapy, Harry just got on with his life and lived every day as if it was his last. He went to school and although he would often come home complaining he had a severe headache, at least he attempted to live as normally as he could. He eventually learned to live with these headaches and he had so much energy for someone so sick, even though he tired easily and loved going to bed early. As a family we lived for three months at a time; it was at quarterly intervals that his scan was due and we would get quite anxious leading up to it, but when we received the results stating that Harry's tumour remained stable, it was like a green light and we breathed a sigh of relief for the next three months at least.

I don't think you realise, until you're faced with the situation, how much of an impact cancer has on someone's life and Harry missed out on an awful lot of the things most healthy children take for granted. I know Harry hurt inside and he did cry a few times, wishing he'd never had the tumour, although he didn't want to let anyone see that and most of the time he would just laugh it off. He just wanted to be like everyone else. I remember one Christmas he had a new bike and he loved it, but he struggled to ride it because of his illness, with one of the side-effects of all the treatments he had received being a problem with his balance.

The treatments had really slowed him down and, while he was so full of energy, he got tired easily, and he found he couldn't do the things he would have liked to have done (like riding that new bike) and I know this affected his pride. If he got tired, he would often lie on my bed or he would look out of the window to watch his brother and all his friends playing happily in the street. I knew he wanted to be just like all of them. Even though he would go to play with them whenever he wasn't tired, that wasn't often enough for Harry. Everyone deserves to see their childhood through but, as much as we tried to give him the best life possible, Harry had effectively lost his childhood to cancer at the age of seven years old when he was diagnosed and that's the really sad part of it. I know the pain that every parent out there who has a child with cancer feels inside; to watch your child go through such an illness is just heart-breaking. You always try to focus on the positives in your lives but the hidden hurt you feel is immense, as you feel so helpless.

If you ever saw Harry during this period you would have known he was ill and suffering from a serious illness, but his outlook on life always remained positive and he was happy in his own little way. We honestly thought the treatment he received had controlled the tumour sufficiently and, while we knew it would never be entirely cured until there was a cure for brain cancer, we thought he would carry on as he was forever.

2

Putting the CAN into Cancer

*'I am incredibly proud to support the HelpHarryHelpOthers
campaign. Harry is an extraordinary young man who has turned his
difficult experience into a quest to help others.'*
Leona Lewis (X-Factor Winner 2006)

Harry was simply a unique person and he had an amazing outlook on life which made him a very special human being. Every day he would put his illness aside and he carried on as if nothing was untoward. He just wanted to be happy and positive and wished every day was full of fun. Any challenge he would face, not necessarily to do with his illness, would just be met head-on and he would deal with it with full-on energy and a 'can do, will do' attitude. He had this very mature way of dealing with whatever came his way. He would tend to step back and look at the challenge facing him; then he would just get on with it and I think that is where his saying 'Make it Happen' came from. Harry didn't focus on his illness, and he never thought of the negatives ('I've got brain cancer, I can't do anything about it and I can't do this or that . . .') but always focused on the positives ('I can still do this …and I can still do that.') He would say things like: 'If I look OK and feel OK, then I am OK.' That sort of outlook and vision on life and the world really gave Harry an amazing ability to reach out and touch people's hearts, from the very young to the very old. Harry always said: 'You've got to put the CAN into Cancer' …and he sure did that.

No child should ever have to know about cancer like Harry did. He knew how it felt but he never once felt sorry for himself. However, Harry did have a fear of dying which I suppose was only natural, even to the extent of having dreams that he was going to die during surgery. He knew that having a tumour was life-threatening but he knew he was OK as long as his tumour stayed the same size. Most of us worry about certain things which happen in our lives and we tend to fixate on the negative side rather than celebrate all the good things life has to offer. Harry had been through an awful lot in his short life but he was so selfless and he was just happy with the fact that we had each other. There would have been no point in me going to pieces and dwelling on Harry's situation – I mean, how could I when he was so chirpy? His beaming smile and the endless laughter he created would light up the darkest of rooms, so as a family we just got on with it, took each day as it came and that's just what Harry did, every single day. The alternative would have been to sit at home and worry about something that might never have happened and let it all turn to bitterness inside. Rather than waste time worrying about it, we decided to live and enjoy every single precious minute with Harry and he sure made every minute count

Harry loved life and treated each day as a new challenge, even if it was just a day spent at home in his pyjamas. He loved nothing more than to throw on his pyjamas and sit at home in front of the TV. Most of us would get bored after a few hours of lounging around at home, but not Harry. He even made such a simple leisurely afternoon fun. I think for us as a family (and given the impact his illness had on each of us) we just enjoyed being together. I didn't care what I did as long as I was with Harry and his brother and sister. Every day was special and the days we spent at home together were particularly special. Since I had to become Harry's full-time carer, I always looked forward to collecting Harry from school and every Bank Holiday or half term felt to me like Christmas because I got to enjoy quality time with Harry. I loved spending time with Harry, his brother and sister and nothing gave me a greater feeling as a mum than being with them. I see my children as my best friends and I genuinely enjoy their company. Harry was my soul mate. We shared fun times, and sad times. We sang together, played, cuddled and he was just my little buddy. We giggled lots every day and although we were going through a terrible journey as a family, I loved my life with Harry in it, although he was so dependent on me and he was with me everywhere. As long as I had my children, I didn't need anything else.

We all knew in the back of our minds how serious Harry's situation was, but with a child whose outlook was so positive, it just helped us through what would have been a dreadful period in most people's lives. When you look around at some people's faces you can see the stress in their eyes and I think the world would be a better place and people would generally be a lot happier if they had Harry's outlook and didn't dwell on all the bad things in their lives and just got on with it. But that's easy for me to say. Life is hard and stressful sometimes, but I always instilled in my children the need to embrace every single day. I tried to teach them that nothing in life is as important as having each other, regardless of what's going on in our lives. As a very normal, working class family, we've always been very proud of who we are, and Harry was no different. Harry wasn't materialistic and liked all the simple stuff in life. He loved just going to the park as a family with a bat and ball or a football and a picnic, or even just time together to chill out. I guess he was an 'old fashioned' kid at heart. He loved treats, of course, but he wasn't besotted by the latest gadgets like a lot of children are today. He knew, even at such a young age, what was important, and that made him very special, too.

It was during the period when Harry was receiving radiotherapy at the Queen Elizabeth II Hospital in Birmingham, towards the end of 2007, that Harry became friendly with a man called Robert Harley and a girl called Rosie (who was around seventeen or eighteen years old) as they were always having treatment at the same time as Harry. One day, Harry got chatting with Robert and his friend, who always seemed to be with him. We later discovered that Robert's friend was in fact his chauffeur, so we obviously thought Robert was some sort of businessman or a millionaire, but Harry wasn't fazed by this and continued to chat to them as he would to anyone else. Harry was a great icebreaker and would always find opportunities to make light of his situation. For example, if we caught him with a finger up his nose he would reply: 'I'm just trying to get to my tumour, mum.' Then he'd laugh it off.

As Harry often got on the table for his radiotherapy treatment straight after Robert, he would sometimes say things like: 'Hello Robert, did you keep the bed warm for me then?' as they passed each other in the waiting room on the way to receive treatment. Harry would just smile and talk to everyone, regardless of age, religion, creed or colour. He'd giggle out loud and just lighten the really subdued mood that hospital waiting rooms are renowned for. After all, everyone was there for the same reason – they all had brain cancer – so it's no wonder the mood was solemn.

The day before their last radiotherapy session on the 14th December 2007, Harry asked me if we could go to the shops to get Robert and Rosie a card and a present. Harry was kind and thoughtful like that. We went to our local shop and Harry saw a couple of cards with angels on, so he picked them up and he also saw a card he wanted to give to the ambulance driver, who Harry always had a laugh and a joke with. Harry had picked these particular cards because they had nice verses inside about staying strong. Harry wrote some touching words inside the cards which said something like:

> *'It was nice meeting you and I hope you stay strong after your*
> *treatment.*
> *Hope we keep in touch.'*

Harry didn't know what to get Robert, given that they didn't really know each other as such, but he picked up a box of Thornton's chocolates as a present. He also bought Rosie a key ring with her name on it. Harry wrapped them up and took the presents into the hospital with him, but he didn't see Robert in the waiting room on that occasion, and he gave them to the nurses so they could give the presents to Robert and Rosie. When he went into the treatment room to receive his last lot of radiotherapy, Harry thought he wouldn't see Robert again. Afterwards, obviously a bit tired from the treatment, Harry was brought back into the waiting area and there was Robert, waiting for Harry with the present and card in his hands. Robert passed Harry his business card and said: 'I don't know what to say, Harry. You've made me really emotional and I feel really humble. What a thoughtful little boy you are. Stay in touch. You must come over to my farm sometime.' Harry was touched by what Robert had said to him and they obviously made a great impression on one another, even though the age gap was enormous.

With the treatment finally over, Harry phoned Robert occasionally to find out when his scan was due and to see how he was doing. The two kept in touch, mainly over the phone and the friendship developed in the weeks that followed. Quite amazing really, for someone so young to become friends with a grown man like Robert, but they did have some common ground after all.

During all their conversations, Harry had never once enquired into Robert's private life. Why would he? During the period they were both waiting for their scans, Robert invited us to his farm in Worcestershire and we took him up on his offer on more than one occasion. Robert had a collection of classic cars, probably about a dozen and, as most boys like cars, Harry was in his element. Harry, being very cheeky and inquisitive, didn't really know what Robert did for a living and asked if he was once a famous footballer or something because he had lots of nice cars. Robert was in fact a director of a large organisation called South Staffordshire Water, so Harry's assumption was way off the mark. As a family who come from the suburbs of Birmingham, we weren't used to the countryside really, but we loved it all the same and Robert's wife Trina took the children out for a drive in one of their open top classic cars, up and down the country lanes. They had the time of their lives.

From then on, the friendship continued and grew stronger for several months. Then one day in June 2009, right out of the blue, we received a phone call from Robert's wife to say that his health had taken a backward step and he had become very sick. The doctors had actually found Robert had developed another tumour in his brain. As soon as Harry had heard of the news, he wanted to go to the hospital to see Robert. Darren and I were in a bit of a dilemma because we didn't want Harry to see Robert so ill – how could we allow a nine-year-old boy to go to hospital to see a man who was really poorly and suffering from the same illness as he was? It didn't seem the right thing to do, even though Harry knew there were so many different types of brain tumour which all had very different side-effects. We kept saying to Harry that what happened to someone else might not be what happens to him and we wanted Harry to understand that just because Robert's tumour was making him really poorly, it didn't mean his tumour was going to do the same. We were being very honest with Harry, as we always were and that was genuinely the case. While Robert was diagnosed with brain cancer it was a completely different type of tumour and was in a different location to Harry's. All we wanted to do was protect Harry from the worry of it, as it was so close to home for him. As a parent you have to try to protect your children from certain things and we just thought that the sight of Robert in that hospital so sick might upset Harry. At that time, Harry was feeling good and his tumour wasn't growing, so we sat Harry down and had a chat to him about wanting to protect him from all of that as it may frighten him and it might put negative thoughts into his head. Harry's exact words were: 'Mum, if I ever got poorly you wouldn't want people not to come and see me at hospital because of how they would feel would you?' Darren and I looked at each other and I then said to Harry: 'You know what? If it really means so much to you, then we can visit Robert as long as you do listen to me because it doesn't mean this is going to happen to you.' We couldn't argue with that sort of reply, could we? I explained to Harry that Robert may look different and be very sleepy or just be different to how Harry last saw him but again Harry replied: 'I don't care. It's Robert and he's my friend whatever.' I guess Harry understood so much more about visual changes in people than we gave him credit for, because of all he had been through himself.

In the end we decided to take Harry to see his friend Robert at the hospital. When we arrived there, Robert was in bed, clearly very tired and weak, but he just looked as though he was asleep, so Harry wasn't scared at all. Some weeks previously, during one of their telephone conversations, Robert had promised Harry that the next time he visited he would teach Harry how to swim, as he had his own swimming pool at the farm. Harry couldn't swim and the thought of being taught personally by Robert was an exciting one. The whole time we were visiting Robert in hospital, Harry just talked and talked to him and said: 'You have to get better, Robert, as you said you would take me swimming in your pool, so come on, you have to keep your promise. The next time I come over you can teach me to swim, Robert, like you promised. I've spoken to Trina and I'm going to come and look after you for the day during my six-week school holiday. I'm going to make you a cake as well.' He just rambled on like that for the whole time we were there, probably an hour and a half. If I'm honest, it frightened me a bit because it was all too close to home, seeing Robert in this state. It could very well have been Harry in that bed. I could see Harry look at Robert from time to time but he just wanted to talk to him and he wanted Robert to know he was there. When Harry told Robert about making a cake for him, Robert turned his head slightly and muttered: 'That's lovely.' Harry said to me excitedly: 'He knows I'm here, mum.' When we had to leave, Harry turned to Robert and said: 'I've got to go now, Robert, but can I give you a kiss?' Robert turned his head and whispered back: 'That's nice.' I was beginning to think that this may well be the last time we would see Robert, as he looked very ill indeed. I knew that the nurses were talking about him going home as there was nothing more they could do for him, but we didn't say that to Harry because that would have really upset him for sure.

All the way home that night, Harry was really quiet in the car, not upset as such but not himself and not very chatty like he usually was. I could see he was thinking about Robert. Seeing him like that probably brought home to Harry his own very real situation. During the short journey home, Harry said: 'Mum, I've just got to do something to get Robert better.' As always, I said we would support him in whatever he decided to do. As soon as we got home, he decided he wanted to make some 'Scoobie key rings', which were made of lots of long plastic laces and were all the rage at the time. Harry wanted to sell them in order to raise money for charity. He had obviously thought about the idea a lot, so, the next day, Harry set about with the intent of making lots of 'Scoobie key rings' which he was going to give away, rather than sell, in exchange for a donation to charity. He intended to send all the money he raised to brain cancer research projects in the UK, a cause obviously close to his heart. However, these 'Scoobie key rings' were taking so long to make he got a bit fed up with the whole process and suggested he wouldn't make enough to fulfil his dream of raising enough money to make Robert better. Harry was very much into art, as he had so much time off school. He filled his time up with drawing and making things, so I then suggested taking Harry to Hobbycraft in search of materials and to gather some other ideas of things to make. I was secretly just hoping to spoil him a bit in the store in order to make him smile and didn't realise he was serious about making things to raise money for Robert on a longer term basis.

When we arrived at our local Hobbycraft we just walked all around the store not really knowing what we were looking for, more searching for inspiration, but all of a sudden Harry spotted lots of beads in different colours, shapes and sizes. As if something had triggered a light in his head, Harry said: 'Mum, that's it. I love them. I can do lots of coloured bracelets for everyone. For everyone who gives me some money to help Robert get better, I'll give them a bracelet as a thank you gift for supporting me and my campaign.' The smile on his face was as wide as an ocean and I can picture him now in the middle of the store, staring at these coloured beads. It was like seeing him on Christmas morning opening his presents. He was so happy and just so excited that his idea was beginning to come together. At the moment that Harry had decided what he was going to do to raise money to help his special friend get better, little did any of us comprehend where Harry's journey was going to end up.

Once we arrived back home from Hobbycraft, Harry went into the garden and sat there all day long making bracelets of all different colours. Harry loved the garden and sitting outside in the quiet on his own. He kept asking me for my opinion after he made each bracelet. Harry then got a pad and sat there working out how many beads were on each bracelet and with a calculator worked out how much each bracelet would cost to make. He was loving it. He made the first one for Robert and we had planned to take it to him at his farm, as he had been discharged by then and Harry wanted to tell Robert all about his new business venture. The bracelet he made Robert was in a very dark green, just like the colour of one of his classic cars. Harry also decided he wanted some posters to be printed and he sat there thinking about what his fundraising campaign would be called. We all sat around the garden table and Harry kept shouting out different names. After about an hour he shouted out: 'That's it, mum – "Help Harry Help Others" – because I am going to need help, so that I can help Robert and other poorly people like me.' It seemed like Harry had it all planned out.

From that day, 'HelpHarryHelpOthers' was born and Harry began telling everyone about his venture – family, friends, his teachers at school and he even approached shops to ask them if they would have a bucket of his bracelets so that if people donated to his cause they could have a bracelet. Harry was so committed to helping to find a cure for Robert and other people in the same situation as him that he just bounced off one avenue of promoting his campaign to another. He cared so much for Robert as he was such an inspiration to Harry, even though they had only known each other for a few months. To me, it just showed Harry's compassion, love of life and love for others, especially his friend Robert. Harry was only nine years old at the time and to be putting every spare minute into this venture was just really overwhelming and truly remarkable.

As a mother, I was so moved by Harry's sheer drive and determination and although it was very early days in his campaign, I could see that Robert had been a major influence in Harry's life for some reason and finding a cure for brain cancer had become Harry's number one passion. A sincere heart-warming and inspiring story had just begun; a positivity which had been created by a little boy, our little boy, because of an unlikely friendship with a grown man who was dying before his very eyes; a boy whose journey would touch the hearts of thousands of people globally, even though it was unbeknown to us or even to Harry at the time.

3

Harry Helping Others

*'Harry literally touched the hearts of people in all
four corners of the globe.'*
**James Phelps (who played Fred Weasley in the Harry
Potter movies and is an Ambassador for HHHO)**

As parents, Darren and I have always encouraged our children to do
whatever they wanted to do in life and I have no doubt they will be
whatever they aspire to be. For Harry, being the youngest and the smallest
in the family, he had to think big and he always wanted to achieve big, even
at the tender age of nine years old. Furthermore, he didn't want to wait until
he left school like most children have to. Oh no. Harry Moseley wanted to
be different and he wanted to do it right now! However, for Harry it was
never about his own achievements or self-proclaim. It was always about
helping others.

Within a few days of Harry starting his campaign and naming it
'HelpHarryHelpOthers' he had made hundreds of bracelets and had
talked to lots of people about his campaign, telling them that he was
going to raise money for 'vital research projects'. Then one day, out of the
blue, we had a phone call from Brain Tumour UK, the leading, caring
charity in the UK committed to specifically fighting brain tumours.
Harry was already fundraising for them at the time but the phone call was
a total surprise. They had apparently heard about Harry and his
campaign, even though it had only been up and running for a short time
and confined to the local area. Brain Tumour UK were having their
annual conference in the Midlands that year and ITV's Central News
wanted to feature a story about a child in the piece they were doing for
the charity. I agreed to the filming and the following day Harry was set to
do his first ever TV interview. He met the Central News reporter Katy
Fawcett and instantly Harry really clicked with her. Central News wanted
to film Harry at home, sat at the dining room table making his bracelets.
Katy also sat at the table for a period of time preparing for the interview
and Harry just sat their continuing to make his bracelets while he was
waiting to be interviewed. Even while he was being interviewed, the
bracelet production didn't stop. Most of the news footage turned out to
be about Harry and his campaign to help others, but they also talked

about Harry's illness, which was quite moving to watch. Harry, as ever, was his usual cheeky self and told me off while the cameras were rolling as I clumsily dropped some of his beads onto the floor. Katy just laughed. She could see his love of life, cheeky persona and compassion for others. Harry grew really fond of Katy and every time he had something big going on he'd say: 'Phone Katy, mum …I hope she can be the one to come and film me.' That was just the start of Harry's campaign and from that first Central News recording, Harry decided he wanted to take his campaign to the next level. He said to me: 'Mum, I want my campaign to be massive. I need to have a think about what I can do.' He'd often wake up in the morning and as soon as he had come down the stairs, he'd say: 'Mum, I've had an idea while I was in bed.'

From that first outing to Hobbycraft, when we were desperately looking for inspiration and then Harry decided to buy boxes and boxes of beads and elastic bands it slowly became a full-time job making and selling those bracelets. Harry said to me: 'Mum, I want the bracelets to be cheap. I want to be able to let people have one if they just give me a pound donation. I want them to have a gift in the colours they like, too. This is my pressie to them for supporting me.' I thought: who wouldn't give a pound to a kid for a handmade bracelet? He wanted people to get something for their money. It didn't feel right to Harry to accept money without people getting a gift in return. He didn't want to just shake a tin and expect people to give money and, although it was hard work, Harry thrived on it. No one will ever understand how grateful Harry was that people liked his bracelets and believed in him. It just drove him on and on with all his fundraising efforts. Harry wanted his campaign to be unique and it sure was, right from the start. Some charities give away a badge (like the Breast Cancer Awareness pink ribbon badges) and Harry wanted people to have a bracelet in exchange for giving him a pound. Harry saw his bracelets as 'presents' for people donating their money as opposed to people buying a bracelet. It was just such a unique concept that evolved from a simple bracelet-making idea.

A few days later, Harry was becoming so confident with his idea that he said he wanted some posters printed, so that he could advertise his bracelets. I asked a friend of mine, Sarah Moss (whom I'd met at a networking event in the past) for help in designing some amazing posters with Harry's cheeky face on them. The next decision to make was to think of a charity to support. I'd previously done a skydive for Brain Tumour UK and it seemed like the obvious choice to support them at that time, especially as the reason Harry was doing his campaign was to find a cure for Robert and other people out there who had brain tumours. Harry was still adamant that every penny of the money he raised was to go to support research projects into brain cancer.

A few days later, my friend Sarah came round to the house to discuss Harry's poster design with us both. While we were talking about Harry and his campaign, she was saying how confident he appeared, especially for someone so young and she was so impressed with him, she jokingly suggested that Harry should do a talk at the networking club she was a member of, called 'The Breakfast Club'. The Breakfast Club was run by BNI, a global networking organisation and I attended these meetings every so often, when I was working. They used to start early, very early in the morning actually. I mean I had to get up at 4.30am to get to the ICC in Birmingham between 6.30am and 7am. At these meetings everyone would basically talk to each other about their work and the services they offered and some good contacts were made over breakfast. When Harry heard about this he immediately asked if he could do a talk there. I think the very mention of a cooked breakfast helped make up his mind, though! I said to him that he would have to stand up in front of a room full of people and do a presentation or a talk. He just didn't seem fazed by the idea one bit. I was taken aback that my nine-year-old boy wanted to do a presentation in front of a load of business people he had never met before and even more so at such an unearthly time of the morning, as he would have to do it before school. I think his confidence had come from watching me prepare my presentations at home for the previous few years. He used to sit with me and became very interested in what I was doing and why I was doing it. From that, he knew what I knew in terms of how to do a PowerPoint presentation, so he thought the rest would be easy for him – that's how much confidence he had. Straight away Harry got to work on the laptop and started putting together his first ever PowerPoint presentation. I sat with him and asked him questions on what he wanted his presentation to cover and he made notes and from that he produced his index of what he would talk about. It was like watching a professional business person in action, but clearly you could tell the innocence and beauty of a child preparing it. He had this habit of sticking his tongue out as he was handwriting his notes; he always did that, just like a lot of children do when they concentrate. There were a couple of little spelling mistakes and grammatical errors in the initial draft but this just added to the beauty of the story. However, we picked these up and corrected them when Harry delivered his speech in a practice run at home.

After seeing Harry's presentation I immediately telephoned Katy at Central News to tell her just what Harry was doing. I was in total amazement that Harry was going to be speaking to lots of 'suits' at a networking meeting, more amazingly before school began. Katy was blown away and spoke to her boss, and she was obviously keen to feature the story. It was soon confirmed that a crew from Central News would be along to film Harry at the ICC doing his first ever presentation.

Harry was so excited and wanted to practise his presentation to a 'mini-audience', so during a conversation with Robert's colleague and close friend Gaynor, Harry was invited into Robert's workplace to deliver his presentation. He wasn't nervous at all and most of all he was so thrilled to see where Robert worked. Robert's organisation was based in Walsall, about 10 miles north of Birmingham, and on arrival, Harry signed in the visitor's book and we were met by Gaynor. She was so friendly and soon became great friends with Harry. He delivered his presentation and she was really impressed with it. He was introduced to the chairman of the company and also got to go in Robert's office and sit at his desk, even though Robert wasn't there. He looked so at home sat there and he said he was going to tell Robert all about his visit to his office the next time he visited him at home. With his practice underway and a seal of approval from Gaynor, Harry was on a roll and I think it gave him a big boost. Gaynor gave Harry a great piece of advice which he always remembered and so when he was often asked if he ever got nervous he'd reply: 'No, but if I do get nervous, I'll just imagine everyone sat on the toilet.'

The evening before the 'big' meeting at the ICC, I asked Harry if he was nervous and he said: 'No, mum. I'm really looking forward to it. Let's go do this …Let's go make it happen!' That showed the amazing confidence he had. The following morning came and Harry was so excited. As usual we sang our heads off in the car on the way to the ICC in Birmingham. We always sang everywhere we went in the car together, but usually Harry would be taking the 'mickey' out of me and my voice. He would always lower his head and look over his glasses at me, just like an old schoolteacher. I knew the expression on his face was saying: 'Mum, you really should shut up.' It was very early in the morning but Harry was always the ray of sunshine that you needed to get your day off to a great start. There was no doubt about it. Harry made my day – every day – so much better than it really was with his charm, humour, infectious smile and personality. He made me want to sing from the bottom of my heart, however terrible I sounded. The love I had for him and for Louie and Danielle was so strong and I think this just oozed out of me. My children simply made my life worth living.

As soon as we arrived at the ICC, people were turning their heads to see this little boy in an oversized tee-shirt and a baseball cap, which was turned the wrong way. They must have thought they were seeing things or still dreaming, as it was only 6.30am. He just walked into the meeting room, then sat down at the head of the very long table as if he was chairing the event himself and chatted to people, strangers, sat next to him, while everyone else mingled. Within minutes of the meeting starting, Harry was speaking in front of not only The Breakfast Club but the ITV cameras who turned up to film Harry for the local news programme. If you can imagine the scene of this nine-year-old boy stood in front of a group of businessmen and businesswomen, wearing a tee-shirt (with half his breakfast down it) and a baseball cap (on the wrong way) giving a speech about his own business ideas. You couldn't make it up. Harry didn't care what he looked like but every one of those people listened to his every word intently. By the time Harry had finished, everyone in the room stopped caring what he looked like and they knew the name 'Harry Moseley' for sure. You could see people were really moved by his speech and everyone commented on the content of his presentation. Harry just thrived on it: he giggled out loudly and I could tell he was really enjoying the moment. He walked around the room talking to people at the end of the meeting, showing off his bracelets, which were displayed on both arms. He was so happy and just great during his interview with the local news team afterwards. He was a natural on the camera. He always talked from the heart and his special friend Robert always got a mention. If he couldn't talk about Robert, he wouldn't talk at all.

With his very first formal presentation now out of the way, I had to take Harry back home to get changed for school and back to reality, but first, Katy was attending the school and doing a piece on Harry raising money for his campaign, in the playground. Don't forget: Harry was seriously ill but he had the sheer cheek and determination to want to speak in front of all the business people at the ICC before a normal school day had begun and that took some guts and determination. It was a lovely sunny day and, as we arrived at school following the breakfast meeting, Harry sat at a table with a bucket full of bracelets by his side. When all the children came into the playground they queued up just to get one of Harry's bracelets in return for their donation. Harry was overwhelmed. The children loved them and that made Harry so proud. After the filming had finished, Harry gave me a kiss and just strolled into school with his friends like nothing had happened that morning. That was also a beautiful thing about Harry. He wouldn't boast or go on and on about all he was doing. When he was at school he just carried on like a regular schoolboy, unless anyone asked about his campaign and then he would talk about it.

Some people let illness affect their minds as well as their hearts, but not Harry. He wanted to carry on and become successful, regardless of any illness he was fighting. He didn't want anyone to feel sorry for him just because he was ill. That, I thought, was staggering. Harry just wanted to do more! His presentation was very informative about his illness, but talked in such a positive way of how that was helping him to help others. I honestly think, regardless of his illness, people were just genuinely blown away by him, his age and his story, together with his compassion for others and his sheer determination to help his friend and all other people going through the same 'journey' as him. From then on, Harry loved doing his PowerPoint presentations and wanted to take what he had just done in front of the Breakfast Club one step further and to realise the potential for what he called a 'schools initiative'. He wanted to do a presentation especially for schools to get children involved, as he knew children would love his bracelets. After all, he was a kid himself, so he knew they would really embrace the idea. He wanted to tell his peers about himself and to get the message across that anyone can achieve their goals they set.

Harry had already received a great response regarding his bracelets, as the children loved them at his own school and he knew every kid would, once he had rolled his idea out, up and down the country. However, he wanted to share his story with them first, so they understood why he made them. He wanted every child to hear his story and wanted every one of them to buy a bracelet. I remember Harry once saying: 'Mum, I'd love to get the children all over the country buying and wearing my Harry bracelets, but there's no way I'd be able to make them all myself. The schools are just going to have to have their own bracelet-making clubs and the children will love making them, too, in their own colours.' That was Harry thinking ahead, as he always did.

Harry set himself a task of writing to all of the local schools first, including his own school, Blakenhale Junior School in Sheldon, Birmingham. Even though he wrote to a lot of schools, he didn't always receive a response but he didn't give in and he would write to them again if he didn't get a response from the initial letter. Harry was a very giving child and said to me: 'Mum, I must give something back to the schools for them to want me there. I need to put in my presentation that every bracelet that the school makes and sells themselves, they'll get 15p for their own school fund.' I couldn't believe for one minute that the schools wouldn't want him there and I began to wonder how anyone wouldn't want to give a nine-year-old boy the opportunity to tell his story in front of children of his own age.

Harry then went about adapting his first PowerPoint presentation he had created for the ICC meeting in order to focus on going in to schools to talk to children about his 'schools initiative' idea. He wanted to prepare the presentation over the school holidays so that he was ready to roll it out after the long summer break, which was just about to begin. The content of his schools presentation was really simple. He started off by introducing himself and telling the children all about his illness and treatment. This led on to his goal, which he told in his presentation:

'When I heard that a special friend of mine called Robert Harley had become really poorly from his brain tumour, it made me really sad, so I decided I wanted to help find a cure to help get Robert better.'

Harry then continued and said that his idea would be to:

'Make beaded bracelets that men, women, boys and girls will like and send all money raised from the bracelets to Cancer Research projects, so that one day there will be a cure for brain cancer and all people like me that live in hope will be better.'

Harry's presentation then went on to outline the result from his idea, which was to:

'Keep raising money and awareness until one day there is a cure. I can't help Robert, but I can keep his memory alive and help other people with brain tumours like me.'

The whole idea of presenting to the children was to try and launch his vision of a 'schools initiative' and Harry's ultimate aims were:

- To raise as much money as possible, specifically for research projects and other brain tumour projects
- To get bracelets into schools throughout the country
- To offer an incentive for schools to raise money for their own funds
- To provide information about brain cancer for schools
- To inspire other children to get involved and do good things themselves
- For children to raise money for a registered charity and their own school fund at the same time
- To help teach children basic business skills.

Harry couldn't wait for the six-week holiday to be over so he could start talking in front of children about his schools initiative.

Within just three weeks, Harry had created his campaign, made hundreds of bracelets, had got them into a few shops and had sold them at his school and also at country fayres during the summer holiday. Not only that, but he had also created the idea for his 'schools initiative' and had worked on a presentation for it. He had attended his first ever breakfast networking meeting and I was just in complete shock at his achievements within such a short space of time. Harry had also been interviewed on local TV twice. All of this was quite amazing really. I thought that if things carried on like this, Harry's 'dreams' could become something really special.

It was only when I heard about a TV competition run by Channel 5 called 'Britain's Kindest Kid' that I immediately thought this has to be for Harry. I thought it could be my way of doing something good for Harry, so I logged onto to the Channel 5 website to register Harry for the competition. His whole story inspired me, even as his mum, and I thought it took a truly special child to do what Harry had started and in such a short space of time. In all honesty, just nominating Harry for this competition felt like a good thing to have done in itself and so, once I'd completed the online application form and entered Harry, I tried to forget all about it. Although I felt better in myself for nominating Harry, I honestly didn't really think I would hear anything else about it, as you tend to hear about lots of amazing stories about what children have done in their lives and Harry's story was just another one thrown into the pot.

Just at the end of that third week of the school holiday Harry was desperate to go and visit Robert at home. I'd spoken to Trina, who explained that Robert was deteriorating rapidly, sleeping mainly, so we made plans to visit Robert on the afternoon of 1st August. However, before we could visit Robert, we had planned to go to a country fayre at Shustoke in North Warwickshire. Harry decided he wanted to set up a stall with all his boxes of beads laid out on the table top, so he could make these bracelets bespoke to order. During a quiet spell, Harry's dad took him round the fayre and Harry bought himself a small teddy bear out of his own pocket money. He had decided there and then that he was going to put the green bracelet he had previously made on the teddy bear and give them to Robert when he would see him later that day. As it was a grim, overcast day and at one stage it absolutely poured with rain, Harry just said: 'Let's just pack up and go home, mum, so we can go and see Robert earlier.' Harry couldn't wait to see Robert and give him his present. When we arrived home, we literally dropped all our stuff off at the house and headed straight back out towards Robert's house. As we got on to the M5 motorway heading towards Robert's house, we received a call from Trina to say Robert had sadly passed away. I had no option but to tell Harry, as he was sat right next to me and he could tell something was terribly wrong, just by my reaction to the phone call. It also meant we had to turn around and go home. He knew before I said anything and he just screamed out: 'What's wrong with Robert, mum. Tell me.' We had prepared Harry for the fact that this might be the last time that he got to see his 'special' friend, as he was so poorly, but he'd insisted he wanted to go to say 'goodbye'. Harry was obviously distraught, so we made our way back home to Birmingham as fast as we could. All I wanted to do was to comfort Harry, but we were on the motorway and couldn't stop anywhere. It was just so horrible. The news hit Harry hard because he thought so much of Robert and he was Harry's inspiration. It was all very sad. In many ways, Harry always loved adult company more than the company of children his own age, but he saw something in Robert he liked, something different and maybe Robert was that person who triggered something in Harry. Maybe it was because he was a successful businessman and Harry wanted to aspire to be like him some day in the future.

Harry was so sad that he didn't get chance to say 'goodbye' to Robert or give him his 'special' bracelet and teddy bear, but we went to his funeral. Harry couldn't miss the chance to say 'goodbye'. In fact, Robert was laid to rest wearing Harry's bracelet which was a really nice touch and something Harry had asked for. Harry, being the thoughtful and kind boy he was, decided to make special black bracelets and sent them to Trina for Robert's close friends and family to wear at the funeral. Harry was visibly distraught from losing his 'special' friend, but he said there and then: 'This is horrible, mum, but I want to carry on making the bracelets in memory of Robert. I know I couldn't help Robert, but I'm not going to stop. I want to help other people with brain cancer, so no one else gets poorly like me.'

In the days and weeks after the funeral I took Harry to visit Robert's grave quite a few times and he would talk to Robert as though he was sat next to him in that waiting room at the hospital. He always took flowers, usually five white roses, one from each of us, and he made a special bracelet to hang from his cross and he always updated Robert on how his campaign was going, recounting all his latest achievements. This really helped Harry try to come to terms with Robert's death. To him, it was all about going to see his 'special' friend and I certainly wasn't going to stop whatever helped Harry. He loved picking the flowers to lay on the grave and would just sit at the side, staring at the headstone. After the initial shock of Robert's passing, Harry became more determined to help find a cure for the dreadful disease which had claimed the life of his 'special' friend. There is a saying that 'every grey cloud has a silver lining' and out of all the sadness Harry was suffering due to Robert's death in August 2009 came the silver lining which was the momentum and the gathering pace of Harry's campaign. Harry had lost a friend but he'd gained an inspiration and he wasn't about to stop.

With the campaign now in full swing, there was no stopping Harry as he decided to write to all sorts of organisations and schools up and down the country and we would go round all the local shops selling the coloured bracelets to anyone who was interested. During the school holidays Harry sometimes got bored and I remember him saying one time: 'Mum, I want to go round and knock on some doors to try and sell some bracelets.' I said to Harry that when I was working in sales I would have to phone up some organisations in order to get an appointment to see them and I tried to explain to him how sales worked. He took on board my advice and so he decided to draft a letter which he intended to give to the organisation he was visiting, introducing him and the concept.

A day or so later, we decided to drive to our local trading estate with the sole purpose of testing out the new approach. Once we'd arrived and got out of the car, we ended up walking round the whole of the estate, knocking on each door. At every organisation, we had the same routine – we would walk into the reception area and the receptionist would automatically look up at me, which was only natural, I suppose, and I would shake my head and point down to Harry, who would then respond to the receptionist by joking: 'She's just the bag carrier and chauffeur. Mum's just come to bring me here.' I could see the receptionist sniggering behind the desk as this confident little kid corrected her assumption. If I didn't need to be there, I'm sure Harry would have done it all by himself, he was that confident. Harry would then carry on and introduce himself: 'Hello. My name's Harry. Would you mind please reading this letter and after you have read it, please pass it onto the person who looks after what I'm talking about?' The letter just explained Harry's story; about his brain tumour; about the bracelets and it also mentioned Robert being his inspiration. Harry never forgot Robert. The letter went on to ask if he could leave a sample bracelet and it asked if he could come back in a few days to sell the bracelets to all of their staff. He wasn't annoying anyone all he wanted was for them to reply to his letter and invite him back in. I think the receptionist of each organisation was staggered by this little nine-year-old boy's gumption and intuition, but that was Harry: always thinking of new ideas and new ways of doing things. If ever there wasn't something in the diary on a non-school day, Harry would make something happen and fill the day with something useful. How could they refuse a confident little boy a return visit?

From those initial enquiries, we were inundated with replies from the organisations who wanted Harry to come back and sell his bracelets to their staff. It wasn't all plain sailing though, because there were times when we ran out of certain colours of beads and we couldn't meet the demand until we had replenished our stocks. It was a lesson learned in stock control and supply and demand, I guess. Obviously, I had to tell Harry how the beads were made (that they were injection moulded from plastic) but he would then search the internet looking for the different manufacturers who made them and then he would write off to the suppliers and even wrote off to some plastic injection moulding companies he managed to find out about. He didn't like to type out his letters at first and he would actually hand write each one because he liked everything to be personal and this was testament to him and his campaign. This is what made Harry such a special child, I feel, and what made his campaign unique. He also handwrote the 'thank you' cards that had been designed by my friend Sarah. Harry insisted all his customers should receive one because he wanted everyone to know personally how much he appreciated their support.

As soon as the holidays were over, Harry was keen to get into the schools and was desperate to share the presentation he'd prepared during the holidays with them. I remember Harry visiting his own school to do a practice run for his 'schools initiative' scheme and he presented it to his head and deputy head teachers. Like everyone else, they were just blown away by Harry's presentation and the content within it. They kindly arranged for Harry to deliver it to his peers in a forthcoming assembly and Harry was so excited at the prospect. It was all Harry's own work and the wording and concept of the presentation was so informative and inspiring, not only for children but for the adults as well.

Following the trial run at his own school, Harry was invited to many other schools to deliver his presentation in assemblies to primary, secondary and even sixth-form students. Anyone who would invite him got a visit from Harry (and me of course, the 'chauffeur and bag carrier'). He loved talking to children and spending time with them and he was happy to answer any of their questions at the end of the session, whatever they were. It was done in such a positive way and the children were always

Harry at the Birmingham 5k run in September 2009.

Bracelets for Robert's funeral – August 2009.

Ready for another country fayre at Shustoke in North Warwickshire.

49

Cool as a cucumber outside Number 10 Downing Street.

Lapland 2010 with Jeremy Kyle.

Harry's headteacher and teacher at school in May 2011.

Back at Number 10 with Gordon Brown accepting another award.

Harry and his heroes – the Dragons at the Children's Champions Awards.

Harry's first ever poster, coinciding with the 2010 World Cup.

Who's a popular boy then? Valentine's Day 2011.

Harry with Ben Shephard at the HHHO launch, May 2011.

Harry with Ben Shephard.

Harry loved magic.

Harry in hospital awaiting his brain surgery.

'Nice to see you, to see you nice...' Harry with Bruce Forsyth at Wentworth.

Selling bracelets outside Asda.

Last photograph of Harry with his big brother and sister.

A mother's love.

Harry and the CEO of Virgin Media.

Early days preparing for a speech.

*Harry at the school Prom, two days before being admitted
to hospital in July 2011.*

Harry and his bracelets.

Harry with the England Footballers Federation in Surrey, February 2011.

Harry with his 'special friend' Robert Harley, November 2008.

With his TwitFam at Duncan Bannatyne's Skydive event, July 2011.

Harry and Louie chilling together.

With RED the Virgin Media mascot.

so engaged in his story. We would sometimes take his radiotherapy mask with us and Harry would pass it around to them and this made it really visual for them. He would get such a great feeling from speaking in front of a couple of hundred children at a time and for someone so young to do that so well is pretty amazing, in my book. He was even confident enough to answer questions at the end of each presentation. He would say something like: 'Thank you for inviting me here today. I really hope you have enjoyed my presentation and I hope you can help me make a difference, so that one day we can find a cure for brain cancer. I am sadly too late to help Robert, but I can help others with your help. I am happy to answer any of your questions.' Children are children and they sometimes don't realise the impact of what they say, but some of the questions were quite direct, such as: 'What's wrong with you? Are you going to die?' Harry was unperturbed by the questioning and took them with a pinch of salt. His response was something like: 'Well, I don't know. I just get on with it and I don't worry about it.' Another common saying he would come out with would be: 'Well, I just get on with it and Cancer didn't know who it was picking on when it picked on me!' That response wasn't just words – he genuinely didn't give in to his illness and, most of the time, didn't worry about his situation. 'What would happen would happen' was his attitude. There wasn't any pretence or exaggeration – that was just Harry. We would always take boxes full of beads with us to the schools and at the end of each school presentation, he would ask the question: 'Who wants to make some bracelets?' Every little hand in the audience went up and it really touched Harry that people were interested in HIS idea and wanted to support him and get involved with HIS bracelet-making idea and HIS charity. He was very humbled by the response, every single time. It was so good for Harry to see all these children become fascinated with what they had seen and to see that he had inspired them, too. Harry found it strange that they wanted to be like him, given that he had this terrible illness, but at the same time, he was inspiring all these children to become better people. If anything, it just drove him on to take his concept further.

After every school presentation, we would sit with the children for an hour or so and would help them make bracelets. Harry loved that interaction. It was his way of helping others and he just embraced every minute of it. What kid at the age of nine or ten doesn't enjoy making things? Even the boys loved it. When we finished, we would leave a box of beads (together with the instructions on how to make the bracelets) with the head teacher so that the school could continue the work that Harry had taught them. It was such a simple idea but it was so effective and the message was so powerful. This was all Harry's own work and he used his own imagination to create the presentation and he eventually took the same message to lots of schools, not only in the Birmingham area but across the country.

Everywhere Harry went, all the children thought: 'Wow, he's poorly and he's only nine years old. If he can do this then surely we can.' From every visit, we would get so much feedback from children saying they wanted to help Harry and to do work like him. To me, it identified a 'need' within children out there to become better people and to do something good. Modern-day children tend to get so much bad press and yet we saw the reverse of it. Children genuinely want to do good things and I'd like to think that Harry helped teach some those children he visited that, regardless of age, wellbeing and lifestyle, you can achieve anything you want to if you are passionate enough about something. However young or old you are or whatever challenges you face in life, if you focus on what you can physically do, with the right encouragement and support you really can achieve anything in life. I really think Harry gave those children the empowerment with the tools he had created to go and do something good and this is why Harry's dreams will always live on. He will always continue to inspire both adults and children alike with his story and the tools that he created for others to grasp. Little did Harry know at the time, but he was sowing the seeds for something bigger.

From the business presentations, the 'schools initiative' idea and several fundraising events, like sitting outside the local Asda supermarket all weekend selling beaded bracelets, Harry's campaign was just becoming huge locally and well known within a very short space of time, just like he wanted it to be! He worked on everything himself, created the ideas himself and was very proud of the fact that 'HelpHarryHelpOthers' was not only becoming a recognised 'brand' locally but was, in the process, helping towards his ultimate goal of finding a cure for brain cancer. Bracelet-making clubs had started up and down the country within schools and Harry was very proud of the fact that the children involved were not only helping him to raise money for the campaign but Harry was also giving them a toolkit to help them raise money for their own school at the same time.

By now, we had stopped using Hobbycraft to purchase the beads and the elastic bands because Harry had found another, cheaper supplier; or rather they found us. Harry had written to all sorts of organisations enquiring about the cost of similar beads to those found in Hobbycraft, in order to reduce his costs. One day, we were approached by a supplier at a country fayre we attended and Harry decided to check out his prices and obtained some samples. As it happened, his offer worked out cheaper than anyone else's, something like £8 for two thousand beads, whereas Hobbycraft charged a lot more, mainly because it was a retail outlet and they had their overheads to account for. Harry even wrote to Hobbycraft's supplier to see if he could get a discount for buying in bulk direct to home, but they replied by saying they would only deliver direct to Hobbycraft stores and that they would have to charge their usual retail price, anyway. Harry decided not to use Hobbycraft but to look elsewhere and he started using the other firm we had met at the country fayre. By this time, Harry's orders were getting really big very quickly and, Harry being Harry, he wanted to please everyone, so he kept taking the orders, regardless of whether he could fulfil them quickly enough. He never let anyone down, though.

At first, Harry only made bracelets of one size – one size fits all – but it didn't take long for him to realise that he could make bracelets for everyone whatever their sex, size or shape; small, medium, large and extra-large. He wanted to cater for everyone and he wanted everyone to be able to buy one. He also wanted to cater for everyone's tastes and colour preferences, including making bracelets in the colours of every football team and for any occasion like the World Cup, or whatever event was happening at the time. Harry didn't want to make the usual rubber charity wristbands as they were all the same sizes and he didn't want to give his customers a limited choice of colours or designs. He also insisted that each bracelet was 'hand made with love for all people with brain cancer'. Harry wanted everyone to be happy. He understood all about branding and once said: 'I need to make some proper, official 'HelpHarryHelpOthers' bracelets that people will hopefully buy so that people 'get' my brand. When people see someone in the street with a bracelet on, I want them to know it's a Harry bracelet.'

Harry sat at home one day, thinking up ideas to please everyone. Even though he was adamant he had to have an official 'HelpHarryHelpOthers' bracelet he was still determined to ensure that everyone still had a choice. Firstly, he came up with a pattern using all the colours of his 'logo' which were blue, yellow, pink, purple and green and laid them out on the table. He then wanted to do something in between the colour sequence so his 'logo' colours stood out. He then had an idea that men would prefer black in their bracelets, women would want clear ones and children or teenagers would like 'glow-in-the-dark' bracelets, which he thought would 'look cool in a night club'. Once he'd had the idea, he laid all his beads out on the table and picked out all the black ones first and threaded two or three onto the elastic followed by the pattern of five colours which signified his 'logo'. It might sound simple but Harry had to work out a pattern that would cater for all the sizes he offered. At first, he couldn't get all the sizes with the same patterns; I don't think anyone realised how much time he spent actually working out how each size of bracelet was made up. What Harry probably didn't know at the time was he had actually created not just a genius idea for fundraising but a business enterprise initiative for children which has the potential to be rolled out all over the country.

It was just after the summer holidays had ended and Harry had started to visit schools up and down the country that I received a phone call completely out of the blue from Matt Etheridge, a producer at the time for Channel 5 News. He was lovely on the phone and told me that Harry had been shortlisted for 'Britain's Kindest Kid' and they wanted to come and make a short film of Harry at his school. As expected, it had completely slipped my mind that I had entered Harry for the competition, but it was a nice surprise to receive the call. I told Matt about Robert and how he had sadly passed away and I explained how Harry's campaign had evolved so much in such a short space of time since I first nominated Harry for the award. Matt was blown away and couldn't wait to meet Harry.

Early in September, the Channel 5 producers came to film Harry delivering his PowerPoint presentation at his own school and then they interviewed him, so that Harry could tell his story in his own words. It was a very moving piece indeed and I couldn't believe how confident Harry was, even though it was only his third time in front of a camera. Harry loved being on camera and enjoyed being interviewed. He was a natural and just seemed so comfortable with it all. Once the filming had taken place and the film had been edited, it wasn't long before it was shown on TV, along with all the films of the other nominees. They were all fantastic children and it would be hard to choose between them, I thought. After the filming for Channel 5, we were soon on our way to number 10 Downing Street as we had been invited to meet the (then) Prime Minister, Mr Gordon Brown, as part of the film for the competition. Harry was so excited, not only about meeting Mr Brown, but to be going to London. Harry made a great 'salesman' and he went to Downing Street armed with two specially made bracelets so he could present them to the Prime Minister and his wife – a brown one for Gordon and a red one for Sarah. I asked Harry why he had chosen those particular colours and he quickly replied: 'Well, the brown one is because his name is Brown and the other one is for his wife and is the colour of the Labour thing' (as he called it). As a bonus, he actually came away from his visit to Number 10 with a donation from Mr Brown to the charity. He enjoyed every minute of his time at the house of the most powerful man in Britain, but my fondest memory was as we were all leaving Number 10. Harry was first to step outside and we were waiting for everyone else to come out to have some photos taken. Harry was just slumped back up against the door smiling and staring up at the towering policeman who stood guard outside the house. He didn't care where he was; it just shone through that no matter all the wonderful things he was doing for others, he was still a cheeky little nine-year-old lad. He loved his first experience of London and, as we left the capital, he waved to it as we got on the train and said simply: 'Bye, London …I will be back' and he meant every single word. When we got home we were glued to the TV throughout that week, watching the short film that Channel 5 had made of Harry. It was played repeatedly, along with the films showing all the other nominees, while the public voting lines were open.

We were later informed by Channel 5 that we would hear the results early the next week and I remember that the following Tuesday, we were at the clinic to receive Harry's scan results when I stepped out of the waiting room for a few minutes so I could check my phone and discovered that I had received a missed call from a number I didn't recognise. I rang the number back straight away and discovered the call was from Matt at Channel 5. My immediate thought was he was calling me to say that another child had won the award, as there were some really amazing stories apart from Harry's. However, the suspense was killing me until the moment Matt informed me that Harry had actually won the public vote and was officially 'Britain's Kindest Kid'. I had tears of joy inside me and was so thrilled for him to be recognised by the public. Matt asked me to keep the news to myself for the time being, as they wanted to surprise Harry in the school assembly the following day. After the call to Matt had ended I composed myself before stepping back into the waiting room to re-join Harry and acted as if nothing had happened. It wasn't long before we were called in to see the consultant. The news was good and Harry's tumour hadn't increased in size, so I was grinning from ear to ear about the two pieces of good news I had received in the last few minutes.

All the plans had been put into place for the following morning as I took Harry to school as usual, knowing that he was going to receive a huge surprise soon. The school had obviously been informed by Channel 5 and had arranged for Harry to sit at the front during the assembly and, unbeknown to him, Darren, Dani, Louie and I had sneaked to the back of the school hall in order to see Harry's big surprise. As planned, halfway through the assembly, the presenter from Channel 5, Peter Lane, burst through the doors to the hall and walked up to Harry and said: 'Harry Moseley, I'm here to tell you that you are officially 'Britain's Kindest Kid''. Nearly everyone in the hall was in tears. Harry looked so shocked and put his little hand up over his mouth. He was completely overwhelmed and stood up and launched himself at Peter and hugged him as he cried with tears of joy. At this point, Harry still wasn't aware that we were in the hall until he had got himself together and he eventually spotted us at the back of the hall. It was just a wonderful sight. Following the assembly, Channel 5 interviewed him and I remember him saying: 'It's just the greatest feeling in the world being 'Britain's Kindest Kid''.

Harry was presented with a lovely glass trophy and a cheque for £1,000 for himself and the same amount to be donated to a charity. With the money he had received, Harry, being the selfless boy he was, decided to give his brother and sister £200 each, which was an enormous amount of money for children. With the remainder of the prize money, he said he was going to buy a playhouse so he could use it as his 'bracelet factory and office' for his campaign. He would name it the 'Harley House' in memory of his friend Robert. He could quite easily have gone out and bought toys or clothes, which he would have been entitled to, but I was so shocked that he had made the decision to invest it in his campaign.

It was amazing to think that in the first week alone, Harry had raised around £3,000 and he was just so determined to increase that figure. We honestly thought that after a couple of months he would have a fundraising total and that would be it. He would at least have 'done something for charity', but no, Harry made this part of his journey and his life and every spare minute he had, he wanted to work on something to do with the campaign. Harry had this great love of life and love of people and his campaign was his enjoyment, his creation, his baby and Harry was so touched by the support from everyone he met. He had certainly 'made it happen' but his work had only just begun.

Harry's school knew just how much his campaign meant to him and now he was officially 'Britain's Kindest Kid' they were really supportive and allowed him to miss some of his lessons in order to go to present to board members at several organisations and at other schools. Without their support, Harry's campaign wouldn't have continued. It was as simple as that.

Within the first six months of Harry's campaign starting, he had attended over 20 events and visited some huge organisations such as BAE Systems, who build submarines in Cumbria. He was made to feel very important there and was fortunate enough to have a tour around the site and also a look inside a submarine that was being made. Other organisations we visited were Truflo Marines who were so blown away with his presentation and his campaign that they gave him a cheque for £1,000 for the charity. Royal Mail, South Staffordshire Water and HomeServe were among the other organisations we visited and we had personal tours at most places.

Harry was just so busy visiting schools and businesses and in the December of 2009, a mere six months after his campaign had started, we had a call from the *News of the World* Sunday newspaper, as they had heard about Harry and his campaign and they explained to us that he had been nominated for a 'Children's Champions' award. They wanted to come to visit us and do a story and take some pictures of Harry for a double-page spread they had planned in their newspaper. A few weeks later, early in the new year and following a public vote, we received the news that Harry had been shortlisted for the award and the News of the World wanted to return, this time to make a short film of Harry.

The film crew arrived at our house at 9am one January morning and they spent the whole day with us. They filmed Darren and me at home, filmed Harry at his school and then followed him off to another local school where he delivered his 'schools initiative' presentation and then filmed him coming back home. The following week we heard the news that Harry had won the award and we had to go to London on 2nd March 2010 to receive the 'Children's Champions' award, Harry's second major award in the space of a few months. This was amazing news and it would put Harry's campaign firmly on the map.

That day came and we arrived in London during the evening, shortly before the ceremony. We were driven to a very posh hotel indeed. The hotel was literally a few steps away from the London Eye and, as Harry walked into the hotel reception, he shouted: 'Hey, you don't have to be posh to be privileged do you?' at the top of his voice. There wasn't much time to do anything other than sit down for dinner with the other finalists and their families and then it was time for bed, as Harry always got tired quite early. The next morning turned out to be another action-packed day and yet another visit to 10 Downing Street to meet the (then) Prime Minister Gordon Brown again. It was becoming something of a habit it seemed. Harry really liked Mr Brown and once again he presented him with another two bracelets. As he was giving Mr Brown his bracelets, Harry said to him: 'Remember me?' Then he told the Prime Minister that he had now raised over £30,000. He was so proud of his achievements and just beamed with delight while he was speaking to his new 'friend', the Prime Minister.

It had been a busy day and Harry hadn't had time for a mid-afternoon 'nap'. Without it, he always got tired during the early evening, so he decided to have a quick 'forty-winks' just as everyone else was getting ready for the ceremony. The event was a very posh affair at The Grosvenor Hotel in Victoria and we were all 'dressed up to the nines'. As we walked down the red carpet, we spotted celebrities everywhere. I was really star-struck if I'm honest, but Harry was cool and just marched up that carpet as if he was one of those famous people himself. He was wearing his favourite pink coloured shirt and was wearing one of Robert's ties that we had to shorten for him. He looked very smart indeed, but he also looked like a proper lad, with his shirt hanging out at the side. That was Harry: just being a very normal little boy. There was a lot of media attention at the ceremony and Harry was stopped by Channel 5 News who wanted to interview him as we walked up the red carpet on the way to the hotel reception area. That made him feel very important and just like one of the many other celebrities. I remember this unreal feeling as we were both being interviewed with Jamie and Louise Redknapp standing in the background. 'Is this really happening?' I thought. All this pomp and ceremony was for us – for Harry, a very normal boy from Birmingham – and it was just something I couldn't get my head round.

Just before the ceremony, while we were in the reception of the hotel, having a drink and surrounded by celebrities, Harry spotted his 'heroes', the 'Dragons' (from the TV series Dragon's Den) and he confidently went straight over to them to introduce himself. Harry had especially admired one of the 'Dragons', Duncan Bannatyne, for a while and he had always wanted to meet him, so he could present his business ideas in front of him, his favourite 'Dragon'. He really wanted Duncan's feedback on his ideas and his vision for the campaign. He wanted advice from a 'real' businessman, partly because Robert had been a businessman but unfortunately hadn't been able to see Harry's campaign get off the ground (though at least Robert had inspired Harry to start it up). Hence the reason why he wanted to speak in front of his idol, Duncan Bannatyne, a self-made businessman and someone who has raised thousands for charity.

About a year prior to the ceremony, Harry had written to the Dragon's Den TV series after seeing an application form online to take part in the show and he wrote on the form something like: 'Would really love to go on the show and do my PowerPoint presentation and receive feedback from the 'Dragons' to see how I can improve it. I don't want any money – I just want advice.' Unfortunately, he didn't get a response from the show. I suspect the producers thought it was a 'joke' application as it was from a nine-year-old boy (as he was then).

Anyway, Harry had the gumption to approach the 'Dragons' that night at The Grosvenor Hotel, even though he'd not met them before and, while he had his 'opportunity' he said something like: 'Excuse me, my name's Harry and I'm ten years old. You're my heroes. I wrote off to your programme to apply to be on Dragon's Den but nobody got back to me.' Harry, who had just turned ten at the time, was looking up through his glasses at the three 'Dragons' – Peter Jones, Theo Paphitis and Duncan himself – telling them off for not responding to his application. The three 'Dragons' stood there laughing and didn't know what to say or do except for: 'Oh you're Harry are you?' As it turned out, they had seen Harry's video and knew all about him, so they were playing Harry up a bit. It was really comical to watch because Harry repeated what he had written on his application form. 'I don't want any money off you; just some advice about my presentation. Just tell me what you think.' Harry loved meeting them and I think Peter Jones asked him: 'Who's your favourite 'Dragon', Harry?' Harry replied as they all smiled at him like a trio of Cheshire cats: 'Duncan, of course'. I don't really think that many celebrities understand just how much of an impact it has on children when they take the time out to speak to them, just like the 'Dragons' did with Harry. This event impacted on Harry in a huge way and added to his strength to just keep 'making it happen' for 'HelpHarryHelpOthers'.

The dinner was followed by the main event, the ceremony, which was hosted by Chris Evans and Amanda Holden. The audience was treated to the short video that The News of the World had made in the January and it introduced Harry, his story, stating that he was nine years old at the time of the filming. When Chris and Amanda called Harry to the stage to collect his award they both confessed that they hadn't paid for the bracelets they were wearing so they each gave Harry a £10 note, which was quite funny. As Harry marched onto the stage to collect his award he was very quick to walk on and say directly to Chris Evans: 'I'm ten now, not nine!' That was Harry. He had to get it right and have the last word. The room erupted with laughter and this little boy who, in the face of adversity, had already achieved so much in just seven months since starting his campaign (and all for the love of his grown-up friend, Robert), now held centre stage at a major event in London. Every celebrity in the room was so proud to wear their Harry bracelet that had been left at their tables for each of them. The ones who took the time to speak with Harry were genuinely touched by him. He was funny, witty and nothing ever fazed him. Everyone was treated equally by Harry and everyone was an equal to Harry, whether they were a celebrity or non-celebrity which was another characteristic that made Harry very special.

When it was time to present the award to Harry, the 'Dragons', who were already on stage, were reminded that they had also forgotten to pay for their bracelets just as Chris and Amanda had forgotten to, so they, too, gave £10 each to Harry, except for Duncan, who at first took out a £5 note, then found a £20 note. Harry couldn't believe his luck as he had made £60 just by going up to collect his award on stage. Harry must have thought it was just so easy collecting money off celebrities! Even though Harry got to meet his heroes, he didn't get the chance to get their advice. After Harry's award presentation, we sat down, listening to all the other nominees' stories which just melted my heart. The night wasn't just about Harry, but it was for the other children who had been nominated. It was a truly inspirational night and I was so immensely proud that my little boy was among them.

Harry met so many famous people that night and also made so many of them laugh. The event was being filmed, as the awards were being televised. At one point, Chris and Amanda couldn't read the autocue and they were trying to say: 'I love these awards. I'll be here next year. Will you be here next year?' But they kept getting it wrong, over and over again. After a couple of times Harry shouted from the table: 'At this rate we'll all be here next year'. The table behind us (which sat TV presenter, Rav Wilding, Blue singer Anthony da Costa and some actors from EastEnders) erupted with laughter again. That was Harry's quick wit and I had that in my life every day – fun, humour and just laughter, when you least expected it.

The following day was a day of surprises before we set off home. Harry ended up being invited to Buckingham Palace, which none of us had a clue about before we arrived in London. He turned up at the Palace in his tracksuit bottoms and a very bright t-shirt (or 'happy colours' as Harry called them). He was there to meet Prince Andrew and, as he always had a stash of bracelets in his pocket, he greeted him with a big smile, handshake and of course a Harry bracelet. Harry was thrilled that the

Duke of York was asking questions about his bracelets and why he made them. He was so sincere and seemed interested in what Harry had achieved. Harry said to him: 'If I knew I was coming here I would have made you red, white and blue ones for our flag.' The Prince replied: 'Well if you send me a red, white and blue one, I will send you a donation for your charity.' Harry was thrilled and he insisted I wrote it down, so I wouldn't forget. As soon as we got home he was on a mission and handwrote a letter to Prince Andrew and duly enclosed his red, white and blue bracelets. Sure enough Harry received a letter back from the Prince along with a donation of £250 for his charity. Harry then wrote again to say 'thank you' and as a gift he put in a lilac bracelet for the Queen. Her Majesty's assistant wrote back to Harry to thank him and enclosed a booklet about Buckingham Palace. For a while afterwards every time Harry achieved something he always wrote to Prince Andrew to update him.

One of Harry's many visits early on in the campaign was to the Black Country Housing Group in Dudley to pitch his campaign to them. We had started to build up a relationship with them as they had helped us personally as a family when we moved house and our central heating system had broken down during the time Harry was undergoing chemotherapy. We were introduced to them through the Npower 'health through warmth scheme'. Harry decided to make contact with them and went to deliver his speech and they loved it.

Soon after Harry had presented to the Black Country Housing Group, I received a phone call from one of their managers to ask if Harry would like to attend a launch event and if he could do a speech on their behalf about our story and how they helped us as a family. Harry jumped at the chance and said: 'It's the least I can do, mum, to say thank you to them for helping us.' These are extracts of the actual speech he wrote and delivered to the Black Country Housing Group in May 2010:

'Hello everyone.
My name is Harry and I wanted to speak here today so hopefully you
will all understand at the end of my talk just how dependant families
like ours are on the 'health through warmth scheme'. All I ask while
I'm talking is that you imagine, if the following happened to you, what
would you do or who would you turn to? I am going to give a little bit
of background before I get to how the 'health through warmth scheme'
helped us just so that you can understand the importance of the work
and support they offer to families like ours.

*Our family life and routine was like most families. My mum had a
good career as a national sales manager and worked full-time days
and my dad worked nineteen years for a company on full-time nights.
We were a working class family but had a nice home and lifestyle; two
cars on the drive and holidays to Europe every year.
Then suddenly, overnight, our family routine and lifestyle fell apart
when I was diagnosed with an inoperable brain tumour. Little did
mum or dad know just how much of an impact this would have on all
of our lives. Not only did they have the worry of my illness but also
they had to cope with the impact on our routine and way of life, as I
had to undergo intensive chemotherapy, which meant a minimum of
three days a week at hospital. Mum had to give up her career
immediately.'*

Harry went on to explain how much of an impact being diagnosed with
cancer had on our family lifestyle. Apart from close family and friends, no
one had known the impact Harry's cancer had on us, because to us it was
irrelevant to tell everyone and it still is. It was something personal to us as
a family. We never revealed everything publicly as we didn't want
sympathy. The impact and lifestyle changes were just something we
couldn't change, so, like everything else, we all just got on with it. All that
mattered to us was the family and as long as we had each other, our life
was as rich as it could have been. To this day, what happened with us as a
family is something I wouldn't want to disclose and, at the time, Harry
would only ever speak about it in full detail in private or, as an exception,
for the NPower 'health through warmth' speeches, as he wanted people to
realise just how important their service was to lots of families just like us
who were going through the same journey. I have shared bits of his speech
here to show you just how selfless and brave Harry was, though. He helped
the scheme so much and in return this would continue to help others in
the future. Due to all the personal stuff that happened as a result of
Harry's diagnosis which people don't know about, I don't think people
will ever realise the full extent of Harry's selflessness. Yes, people think he
was 'special', but Harry, Louie and Dani are more special to us than anyone
will ever know. Harry's speech outlined everything the Black Country
Housing scheme had done for us. Here's the final part of it:

*'As mum had to give up work, we had to move house. I know mum
was really worried, as I was constantly in and out of hospital due to
the chemo because I had no immune system and my body was*

neutroplenic. One week or so after moving into our house, our central heating system broke down. Someone had told mum about a grant scheme through another company, but when mum rang, they advised that we would not qualify as it was not my mum or dad who were ill. They did, however, pass our details on and we had a call from Jane Millard from Black Country Housing who told us about the 'health through warmth scheme'. As she was aware of our situation and that we had no source of heat at all, she arranged for an engineer to come out that very day to try and fix our central heating. He advised us that our system was so old and had so much wrong with it that we needed a complete new boiler and seven radiators. 'Health through warmth' helped mum complete all the paperwork at our house and within a couple of weeks we had a whole new central heating system installed under the scheme.

Mum says that she will always be eternally grateful to 'health through warmth' as she really believes that without their help at a time when we needed it the most, we would not be here together today. Please just think about how many families are out there like us, with their world shattered overnight because of serious health and even life-threatening illnesses like mine. Without this scheme, what would they do? Without the 'health through warmth scheme', people with genuine health problems have their only lifeline taken away.

Many of you here today look like important business people. If you suddenly could not work because your child become ill like me, just think …what would that mean to your family? We never ever thought our family would be in this position and are just so thankful to a wonderful scheme such as 'health through warmth' for helping our family and all those that urgently need help.

Thank you.'

Harry subsequently spoke for them in Birmingham and in London and even delivered a speech supporting the scheme at the House of Commons to an audience of MPs. He told them about himself, his illness and the side-effects of chemo and just how important the 'health through warmth scheme' was and how it helped our family. In the weeks that followed, Harry helped them win awards and he became (in my eyes, anyway) an extension of their team. This had nothing to do with his own charity or his campaign, but once again it showed that Harry was 'helping others'. If he thought he could make a difference, he would put himself out there and would happily do what he could to help. This is where Harry was unique. He wasn't only interested in his own campaign but he was just interested in making a difference and supporting other campaigns and other people. You wouldn't get a lot of other charities uniting like that to work together – this is how it should be, though. Overall we all have the same goal, but sometimes, rather than trying to stand out and be the best on your own, if you unite and work together as a team you can have a greater impact collectively and a better result.

4

Making it Happen – Harry Style

'Nothing was too big for Harry. Nothing was too small for Harry.'
Ben Shephard (TV presenter and an Ambassador for HHHO)

Twelve months into the campaign and the summer of 2010 was quieter for Harry. We had to recover from so many personal changes in our lives due to Harry's illness, which had meant we had to move house. We moved in the July of 2010 to a house right opposite the children' secondary school which we hoped Harry would attend, too. We thought it would be perfect as it would allow us to 'cut the apron strings', so to speak, and allow him to go to school alone. We always had huge concerns with Harry and his vision. As I've mentioned before, what he could see was perfect, but he had real problems with his field of vision and that was where Harry could put himself in dangerous situations without realising, as he couldn't see things low down unless he really tilted his head in a specific position. For us to allow him to have some freedom and feel like any other kid going to secondary school would have meant the world to us as parents. We knew he was really looking forward to it. I don't know if I had a premonition though, but I remember talking to lots of friends and Harry's brother during the last term of his last year at primary school and telling several of them: 'I just can't see Harry going to secondary school.' I don't know why and I don't know if it was because I feared that Harry might be bullied about his weight issues. Like everything in life I didn't get it and I had a vision it wasn't going to happen. At the time I was thinking all of this, Harry had been well in himself and had no issues with his tumour. It was strange that I was thinking like that and I often look back and wonder about why I had those thoughts, but I just don't have the answers and I never will.

The summer shows and fayres that we had been to the previous year were impossible for us to attend as we moved into the new house. However, it was a World Cup year and, like many other festivities such as Halloween, Christmas, Valentine's Day, etc., the World Cup was no different and Harry always came up with some special bracelets for those events, too. For every festivity, Harry had special posters done of him dressed up for that particular theme and for the 2010 World Cup he had a giant England hat on. It towered up from his head and there was a great beaming smile on his face. Harry sold loads of the World Cup bracelets, but we also were left with a stockpile of them when England were knocked out by Germany!

No sooner than we had settled into our house, though, Harry was thinking he wanted his campaign to go to the next level and decided he wanted to partner up with another charity in the hope they could help his campaign and they could work together as a 'team'. So in October 2010 we approached Cancer Research UK and they duly sent three of their representatives from London to come and talk to us about Harry's campaign. Harry wanted to do his presentation as it told the whole story and all that he had achieved. We then just chatted to the three people from Cancer Research UK and Harry got on really well with them. He really wanted to support another charity for the next 12 months and we all had a good feeling about Cancer Research UK. Truth be known, Harry always wanted to develop his own registered charity, but I always had at the back of mind that one day Harry might have had enough of his fundraising work and would want to give it up, or his health might deteriorate. Therefore, I explained to Harry that not becoming his own charity at that point meant he wouldn't be under any pressure if he suddenly wanted to stop. While Harry was happy to 'help others' I, of course, was happy to support him but I didn't want him being under any pressure whatsoever. He still 'called all the shots' so to speak and it was Harry who would drive his own campaign forwards. If he didn't want to do anything or go anywhere, he didn't have to. It was completely his call and if he was tired, he would stop. With that in mind, Harry decided to support Cancer Research UK for the next 12 months. It was a an easy decision to make, really.

Cancer Research UK also worked in partnership with Seve Ballesteros, the famous golfer who started 'The Seve Ballesteros Foundation' after being diagnosed himself with a brain tumour. When Seve heard of Harry's work, he invited us to attend his charity event, 'Viva La Vida', which was held at Battersea Evolution, in London. Harry was asked to deliver his first speech for Cancer Research UK. Harry was delighted to be attending and he was so excited about meeting a superstar like Seve. Harry had delivered so many speeches in the past he wasn't fazed by it at all and it didn't matter who he was presenting to, either.

Harry was thrilled to be going back to London again. When we arrived at the hotel, we checked in and Harry had a rest for a few hours. We knew he wasn't due to speak until about 10pm, so it was going to be a long night for him. When we stepped outside the hotel, our car arrived promptly and

Harry thought it was wonderful that a car had his name written on a sign in the window. He was also happy as it was behind a car saying 'Ben Shephard'. For most little boys of his age, it would have been too much to comprehend, but not for Harry. He was loving every minute of it. When he got in the car and saw there was a uniformed driver, he said: 'Now, mum, that's what you call a driver.' He was of course comparing the driver to me, as he always told everyone I was his 'bag carrier and chauffeur'. When we arrived at the venue, we heard the news that Seve sadly couldn't be there himself, as he had received some bad news that his tumour had got progressively worse and he wasn't well enough to travel from his home in Spain. That made Harry really upset, but he was determined to do Seve proud and asked if he could record a video message that could be sent directly to Seve after the show.

Even before the other guests had arrived, Harry marched onto the stage for a sound check and was quite happily shouting 'one, two, one, two' and giggling at the top of his voice, as if he was the show's director. Ben Shephard then arrived and introduced himself to Harry. They sat at a table and laughed and chatted and just got on really well. Ben obviously knew of Harry and was so warm towards him and was just genuinely interested in him and his story. They talked about anything and everything and, at one stage, Ben was quizzing him about girls. It was so lovely to watch and Harry really, really liked him. After all the sound checks and last minute spot checks, Harry got to sit and watch the gymnastics troupe 'Spellbound' do their final practice before all the guests arrived. He loved watching them and was amazed to be meeting them.

As a spectacular night got under way, Harry was sat next to Stephanie Moore, Sir Bobby Moore's widow. Again, Harry being Harry, he just chatted away and they both commented on the very fine cuisine that Harry didn't appreciate the look of (after all he was only ten). He wasn't fussy in the slightest where food was concerned, but he thought it looked so fancy he just didn't know where to start.

Just before Harry's speech, Ben announced that Seve was sadly unable to attend and that he had sent a personal video message to all the guests. Harry watched it and afterwards he leant over to me at the table and he said: 'Mum, that's really touched me. I feel sad.' Not long after, Harry was up on stage to deliver his speech, but I think the emotions of the evening, what with Seve's sad news, just got the better of him. As I've mentioned before, Harry never got nervous and in fact, the larger the audience the more Harry was in his element. He had, after all, spoken at over forty different events by then. However, that night was different. Harry was saddened to hear that anyone was going through the same as him. The news about Seve hit him hard and he didn't appear to be himself. He started so well, talking about himself, his illness and his campaign, but when he got to talk about his friend Robert – the bit he always loved talking about – I could hear his voice shake. He got upset about three quarters of the way through his speech and Ben gave him a huge hug and helped him finish it. Harry was amazing that night and he helped to raise a staggering £53,000 for Seve's foundation, yet he was so disappointed in himself. Everyone was in awe of Harry on that evening and all he had achieved. Stephanie Moore even gave Harry her mobile number, which went straight onto his phone (my phone) as 'Mrs Moore'

As Harry was so tired, we left soon after his speech and just as we were leaving, Darren Clarke, the golfer, made a point of wanting to be introduced to Harry, so Ben Shephard took Harry over to meet him. He said he thought Harry was incredible and his speech had really touched him. To me, that night again demonstrated the sensitive feelings and compassion that Harry had for others and everyone in the audience felt that from Harry, too.

At the time when Harry had the idea of making bracelets for everyone, he wasn't really using Twitter, as he couldn't really get to grips with it at first. It was Ben Shephard who encouraged him to use Twitter during that Seve Ballesteros event. Ben said to Harry: 'Twitter's really good, H. You must Tweet me some time. I'm going to Tweet everyone that I'm here with you and you've done this marvellous speech.' Harry gave Ben a huge hug and when we checked out of the hotel the following morning, Harry left Ben a handwritten note that said: 'It was great to meet you, Ben, and I hope we stay in touch.' He left his (my) mobile number at the bottom of it and added: 'PS. Save some of the girls for me.' From that day on, because of Ben, Harry became obsessed with Twitter and I didn't get a chance to use my phone again, because Harry was constantly using it for Twitter. I remember quite a comical radio interview Harry did with the Birmingham radio station, BRMB (now Free Radio), and their sports presenter, Tom Ross, was talking to Harry about Twitter when Harry said: 'Mum's phone is now my phone but shhhh, don't tell mum.'

Sometimes I wondered whether Harry secretly knew his life would be short, as he wanted to get as much out of it as possible and do as much as he could in the short space of time he had on this earth. In the October of 2010, we were contacted by ITV and a producer from The Jeremy Kyle Show as they had seen an article about Harry and they were about to produce a show about inspirational people and they wanted Harry to appear on the show. As is happened, it was another one of Harry's dreams to tell his story sitting on a sofa on a TV show, so he could raise the awareness of brain cancer on national TV. We agreed for Harry to appear on the show, so we had wait for the producer to contact us to arrange a time. They had obviously done their homework as they knew all about Harry's story and thought he was amazing. The producer called us back on the Wednesday and asked us to go to Manchester on the Friday of that particular week and said they would contact me to arrange transportation for Harry and me to travel to Manchester. This caused a bit of a problem because the times they wanted us to be there (between 1pm and 3pm on that Friday) coincided with Harry's quarterly scan at the Birmingham Children's Hospital and that I couldn't cancel. The scans were of the utmost importance, because they effectively gave us another three months breathing space if it was positive (which they all had been) and more time spent with Harry. At no time would we ever have cancelled the scan, even for an appearance on national TV.

Harry had actually written to many other TV shows (in order to tell his story to a wider audience) before he received the call from The Jeremy Kyle Show but to no avail. The fact that ITV had actually contacted him and now he couldn't go because he had to have a scan hurt Harry even more than it might otherwise have done. It was another blow for Harry, as he had been let down a couple of months before by The Michael Ball Show. Again, a similar situation prevented Harry from appearing on national TV, except that time we had already planned to go away when they wanted Harry to appear on the show and I had to let Harry down. I emailed the show to thank them for taking an interest in Harry and asked if they could let us know if any other openings came up. They replied to say that they would contact us as soon as we returned from holiday to arrange another date, but unfortunately, nothing further happened. Of course, as adults, we understand about disappointments and the media is so fast-paced and you usually only get one chance, but when you're dealing with children, it's hard to explain to them about all of that. So Harry was understandably disappointed and felt let down.

I immediately rang the producer of The Jeremy Kyle Show to say that Harry could go on the show but he would have to go to Manchester after his scan which was first thing on the Friday morning. For whatever reason, I think the timing issues etc., it all fell apart and Harry wasn't going to get to sit on the sofa telling his story. I was dreading telling Harry the disappointing news, but after school I plucked up enough courage to tell him and he was obviously quite upset, because it was his dream to appear on the show and he was getting all prepared for it. Harry didn't want to be famous, it was just that he wanted to tell his story and to tell the world about Robert and also to spread the word to the big, wide world. Harry had got so excited that I think he had already told his friends at school he was finally going to tell his story on national TV, but now his dream had been shattered again; this time because he had to go for a scan.

Surprisingly, I had a call the next day from the producer of the show and she said that the show's production team had been thinking of an alternative for Harry and they had come up with the idea of inviting Harry to Lapland for a special Christmas show they had planned. The producer wasn't guaranteeing anything and stipulated that it was only an idea at that stage. She made a point of asking me not to mention anything to Harry, just in case it didn't come off. The only downside was that there would only be two tickets available. With all that the family had been through and all the lifestyle changes we had encountered, there was no way we could afford another three tickets for Darren and the other two children to come along. As parents, we were in a really awkward situation now, because if this did come off, we were really worried about his brother and sister's feelings about being left out. This was what they all deserved – not just Harry who was at that age where he would just love it and find it magical. If I had thought for one second that Danielle and Louie would have been upset at not going with us, then I would have decided not to go and Harry would have been none the wiser, but when I explained the situation to them, they immediately encouraged me to take Harry and I was so touched by their reaction. They knew Harry deserved to go for all he had been through and it was testament to the kind of children they are. They themselves, whose lives had also been drastically affected by Harry's illness, had the biggest hearts and encouraged me to take Harry. Darren and I obviously made it up to them though and treated them, so they didn't feel completely left out.

A few days later, ITV confirmed that the trip had been all arranged and I was asked not to tell Harry anything as they were planning for it to be a big surprise. On the day we were due to travel, I had to pack Harry's case with winter clothing without him knowing and without giving away the big secret that we were flying to Lapland to meet Santa and that he was to be filmed for a special TV show. The story I told Harry was that he had been invited to speak in front of the Manchester Education Department about his schools initiative. A few weeks beforehand, he had spoken in front of the Birmingham Education Department and I made out that word had spread to Manchester about his plans to roll out his initiative to schools across the country and they were keen to meet with Harry. He was thrilled to bits to hear the news but little did he know that the real reason he was travelling to Manchester was to appear on The Jeremy Kyle Christmas Special.

We arrived at the hotel in Manchester and as a treat I suggested we go ice skating in town, knowing that Jeremy Kyle would make an appearance at some stage and, again, I had to keep the plan to myself. So, as soon as we had set foot onto the ice rink, Harry spotted Jeremy Kyle interviewing a little girl, who was stood not far away on the side of the rink. As it turned out, the little girl was suffering from Leukaemia and she was also part of the 'set up', but at that stage, Harry still had no idea what was going on. Jeremy appeared at the side of the outdoor ice rink and pointed a microphone towards the little girl and said: 'Hello, are you Adele? Do you know who I am?' The girl looked at Jeremy and shook her head. Jeremy and the film crew then headed over towards Harry and said: 'Are you Harry? Do you know who I am?' Harry didn't hesitate in replying: 'I know who you are. You're Jeremy Kyle.' With the cameras rolling, Jeremy said to Harry and Adele: 'Tonight, we're going to give you an amazing trip of a lifetime and we're taking you all to Lapland.' Harry looked at me, looked at Jeremy then looked at me again, grinned at me and said: 'Mum, I'm never going to believe anything you say again.' Harry was genuinely surprised and shocked and of course happy. It was an amazing feeling to see his happiness and the surprise on his face.

Harry seemed to hit it off with Jeremy right from the first meeting on the ice rink in Manchester and the one thing Jeremy liked most about Harry was his loveable personality. I remember Jeremy saying to his production crew at 4am before we boarded the plane to Lapland: 'Come on, let's go and have a cigarette before we board the plane.' Harry heard this and he butted in: 'Yeah, come on then, Jeremy. Let's go outside and we'll have a cigarette and, when we get to Lapland, you can buy me a pint.' To hear words like that coming out of a ten-year-old was so funny. From that point on, Jeremy just loved Harry. That was Harry to a tee. A grown man in a little boy's body. It was the little amusing comments that made him the person he was – very quick witted and funny. He always reminded me of a miniature Peter Kay.

From the time we arrived in Lapland to the time we arrived back, Harry loved every minute of his special trip of a lifetime. He smiled and giggled the whole time. We spent four days in Lapland. The first day we spent on our own and did our own things, like sledging and walking around the town, but the second day there was a lot of filming to be done. Harry thought he was going to tell his story on that day, but the idea of the show was to find out about his illness more than anything else and that was very emotional in itself. The third day was the fun day. Harry loved it and wanted to be in the snow all the time and we went sledging most of the day and he didn't care if he fell into the snow. He would fall back and just lay there stretched out. He looked so carefree and happy that day, you wouldn't think there was anything wrong with him. He didn't moan or whinge once and embraced every second of the trip. The last day in Lapland involved a full day of filming and Harry spent a lot of time with Jeremy and the other children. They all had reindeer rides and met Santa Claus and that was all being filmed. There was a lot of hanging around that day as you'd expect for any TV show, I guess, and it was tiring for the children. There was a four or five hour wait to go and meet Santa but, when Harry's time came, he had to give Santa the letter he had written, which explained what he wanted for Christmas. Most children probably put the usual things like a bike, Xbox or iPod, but when Harry sat down next to Santa, Santa read through his letter to himself and said: 'Now, Harry, let's look at your letter then.' Santa turned to Harry and asked him what he wanted for Christmas and asked him to read out his letter. The letter read something like:

'Dear Santa,
I know you probably can't do this for me but all I'd really like for Christmas is a cure for brain cancer. I know it might not be possible and I'm working on it anyway, so if you can't sort it, can I have a bike as I've always wanted a new bike?'

Well, as soon as the words came out of Harry's mouth, I was in floods of tears. I was wearing a big padded ski suit and I buried my head inside it and hid my face from the camera. Jeremy had to walk away as he was moved by what Harry had said. As much as I was there with Harry, every step of the way, I didn't know how that moment felt for Harry, trying to explain to Santa that he wanted a cure for brain cancer. I've no idea what Santa thought of Harry's Christmas wish but he had us all in tears. As a mother, you're there for your children to love them and protect them. If they're poorly, you patch them up and make them feel better and reassure them. I could do all of that but I couldn't make Harry well again. That, as a parent, is the worse feeling in the world. Knowing you can't do anything to make them better. All I could have done was to be there for Harry, but even that didn't feel enough. It definitely wasn't enough; even what the doctors had done wasn't enough. For Harry to say something like that just shows the amazing qualities he had and the sort of person he was, even as a ten-year-old and it was things like that which backed up the fact that Harry was an incredible person. It wasn't just that one-off event. That trip to Lapland summed up Harry's personality, though, and how he was really feeling inside. The trip finally came to an end and it was back to 'normality' for Harry and his campaign, but I will never forget those few days.

I see lots of campaigns for children being started up, which is great but most of them are started and run by the parents. Everything Harry did, though, was started from his own heart and from his own selfless ideas and he put those into action himself. Yes, I supported him and advised him, but it was all inspired by Harry. I never realised at the time how much Harry actually helped me as a person because for me, it was my only way of helping Harry. By working on his campaign and supporting him, he kept me focused and positive all the way through and kept me thinking that what we were doing would one day possibly help find a cure for Harry and indeed brain cancer itself.

There were many instances of Harry interacting with people he didn't know but wanted to help. Harry was contacted by a 'make a wish' organisation but he wasn't interested in making a wish for himself and kept fobbing them off. He didn't want anything from anyone really. Harry was more interested in giving back to people. Anyway, there was a little boy he had followed on Twitter. I think his name was Leighton Cook. He was about two years old at the time and Harry was in touch with him. I remember one day Harry told me about Leighton and how he had a brain tumour and how it really saddened him. Harry wanted to do something nice for Leighton. So when this 'make a wish' organisation contacted Harry again, he just told them to give his 'wish' to Leighton. That was Harry; always thinking about others. I believe the organisation got in touch with Leighton's parents via Twitter to discuss him having a 'wish', all thanks to Harry. Harry also had saved up £8 and, knowing Leighton liked Peppa Pig, he got me to take him to the shops to spend his money on Leighton and we sent Leighton his present by post. I honestly think Harry was more selfless than people will ever realise. There were just endless examples of how kind and considerate Harry was towards other people going through the same journey as he was.

Over the Christmas period and early into the new year of 2011 Harry was busy behind the scenes writing up his new website information for his partnership with Cancer Research UK. He really wanted to get it up and running quickly, but due to lots of red tape, things were dragging on a little and it frustrated Harry. However, in the February, the England Footballers Federation (EFF) were due to launch their own charity and they specifically asked for Harry to attend to tell his story as the charity would be supporting Cancer Research UK along with Help For Heroes. Harry jumped at the chance and asked if he could take his big brother with him, as he knew Louie was a huge football fanatic and would love the opportunity to meet some of England's best footballers. The event took place in Surrey and it was really a media event more than anything else. I think there was every newspaper and TV station there, including Sky Sports. Harry took some red and white England bracelets along with him and gave them out as gifts as he arrived. Then he went off on his own to meet Frank Lampard and John Terry before having to do the formalities.

Once the event got underway, Louie and I sat in the audience and Harry, along with a man from Help for Heroes, sat at a table with Frank Lampard and John Terry. Before the event started, a female presenter from Sky Sports who was hosting the event asked Harry who he supported. At the time he 'liked' Everton, all because of a match he had attended previously. He loved the atmosphere there, so he decided to support them. The truth was Harry didn't have a great interest in football unless it was England or his brother Louie was playing. I think he just didn't connect with sport at all because of his illness and tiredness. He also liked Birmingham City but that was more because he wanted them to be proud of him and get behind his campaign. He was so proud of the 'Blues' bracelets he made and wanted every fan to have one.

When it was Harry's turn he got up and delivered his speech to Frank, John and the media and he spoke about the work that Cancer Research do and how important it was to find a cure for brain cancer. He also told them about Robert, of course, and all about his campaign that he had started himself, so they understood why they were given an England bracelet. They all seemed really touched by his story. After Harry sat back down next to Frank and John, the Sky Sports producer said: 'Who do you support, Harry?' Harry quickly replied, being sandwiched in between Frank and John: 'Err …No comment,' and laughed. She knew and prompted him again. He said: 'England.' He knew what she was getting at and he was being a 'cheeky Charlie'. When she asked again – 'Come on you can tell us' – although Harry didn't realise that Chelsea were playing Everton the next day, he looked up at the ceiling and said: 'Everton'. The producer then said: 'Oh, Chelsea are playing them tomorrow, Harry. Who do you think are going to win?' Harry didn't care who was sat next to him.

He just blurted out: 'Everton, of course,' with a huge grin on his face. The whole room was laughing, as only Harry could get away with that, especially being sat next to two such famous Chelsea stars.

Afterwards, Harry and Louie talked with Frank and John and they had photographs taken together. Harry was so proud that they both wore his England bracelet. Harry had his own little printed storybook about his campaign and all the England footballers signed it for Harry to keep, along with an England shirt which they also signed. Harry treasured the book and it became a very sentimental piece. This day was a special day that started a genuine friendship and Harry gained support from John Terry, who was really moved by Harry's selfless story. Following his speech, Harry built a relationship with the EFF and was their first 'hero' on the official website which meant so much to him (and he still appears on it today).

Not long after the launch of the EFF, England were playing at Wembley and John's agent got in touch with us and asked if Harry could send 50 England bracelets out to reach John Terry by 9am the following morning. Although it was late in the afternoon Harry's reply was: 'You bet.' We hurried home and got to work making the bracelets. We rushed them to the Post Office and Harry was so thrilled to hear that John had received them in time. He was even more thrilled when one of his Twitter friends commented that he had seen the England footballers wearing Harry's bracelets on TV. He was just beaming inside and out and was quite rightly so proud of himself. He even put the TV on and took a photo of the screen showing the England players wearing his bracelets.

Harry became very fond of John Terry and spoke to him a few times over the phone following the EFF launch event. Personally, I think John is a really sincere family man whom I will always be eternally grateful to for his friendship. He's someone that Harry was very honoured to meet and someone that Harry knew had a heart of gold. While a huge personality and a successful footballer, he's a man who has kept in touch with the reality of what's important in life. I don't know how, but Harry knew all the genuine people that were out there and was so humbled by all those who supported him.

Harry wanted all the money he made from selling the bracelets to go to a particular charity and that charity in the second year of his campaign was, as I've said, Cancer Research UK. Harry particularly wanted to help fund their life-saving work into the causes, diagnosis and treatment of brain cancer. Harry's involvement with Cancer Research UK officially began with the launch of the 'HelpHarryHelpOthers' website in May 2011.

He had been waiting three or four months, but when it did finally go live, the orders came pouring in. Harry was completely blown away by the response and we were so busy getting them out, we didn't find time to do anything else it seemed. My lounge turned into a cross between a production area and a Royal Mail sorting office but Harry just loved it and he'd often put some of the pictures of all the orders he was bagging up and posting, on Twitter. With the orders mounting up and all the school speeches and presentations we were both flat out, but Harry just wanted more and more of it. The decision to join forces with Cancer Research UK had been a good one, it seemed.

A process was created for the orders to be sent through from Cancer Research twice a week and he always updated his 'Twitfam' about how many bracelets had been ordered in each batch and how many he had made. He just liked to tell people what was going on and share his news, both the ups and downs of his life.

Once the campaign really took off, Harry started to take a lot of notice of how different organisations used advertising slogans such as 'Cancer Research UK – Together We Can Beat Cancer' and how they used them to convey positive messages. He always tried to find some positives from his cancer and would relay this positivity to his beloved 'TwitFam'. I remember my grandma used to tell me, every time I doubted myself, to 'put can't in your pocket and pull out try' and Harry looked at that saying and used it in his campaign as a positive message to give his followers in case they were to doubt themselves at any time. There was a lady on Twitter that Harry would 'chat' to who had cancer and he would say to her things like: 'Well, just smile. If you smile the world will smile with you and you will feel happier. Just put the CAN into cancer.' Harry really gave a sort of 'wakeup call' to some of his followers who were going through a rough time with cancer by writing things like: 'Do you feel OK? Do you look OK? Then you are OK. Smile your way through the day.' Harry always smiled. For someone who doesn't smile a lot and for them to read something like that from an eleven-year-old boy, the only response you'd expect is a positive one, because the way Harry put it across made the recipient respond in the same way. His philosophy was that, if you can smile your way through life, then it makes you feel a whole lot better, regardless of what's wrong with you. He would Tweet lines like that most days and for the person on the other end to read something like that first thing in morning, it must have started them off to a good day, regardless of any illness or stress they were suffering in their own lives.

Harry seemed to create smiles every single day for all of his followers on his Twitter account (@Harry_Moseley), (which I have now taken over as it was my last promise to him to update all of his followers). I remember some of the comments he would put on Twitter and he would just brighten up everyone's day, no matter how dark, miserable or wet it was outside. He would 'chat' on Twitter to some people who had a similar disease to him and he had this amazing ability to put people's lives into perspective. I don't really know how he did it, but I guess it was a 'gift'. He created names for every day of the week and it got people's days off to a great start. He would open the day with one of the following, according to what day it was:

#morishmarvellousmonday
#terrifictuesday
#wowzerwednesday
#thrivingthursday
#feelgoodfabulousfriday
#sensationalsaturday
#supersunday

Harry also came up with #SelflessSaturday. He wanted this to be a day where everyone around the world would do something good for someone else, even if it was just for half an hour. He really wanted other people to feel like he did inside and it was something he was planning to roll out as a 'project'. He had so many dreams he wanted to get into place and I was determined to help him achieve this. He also invented #twitpoemfestsunday, too, and tried to get his Twitter followers tweeting poems on Sunday afternoons. Harry loved poems and would often tell his 'Twitfam' just how much he thought of them, through his poems. Here is a selection of poems he wrote while he was ill:

'Help Harry Help Others
Is my special campaign
To help all people
like me with a poorly brain.'

****

'Cancer, you can try,
But I'm never giving in,

My aim in life is
To win, win, win.'

****

'*I'm Putting CAN into Cancer,*
I'm fighting everyday,
Trying hard to help others,
In my own special way.'

'*It's #twitpoemfest Sunday,*
C'mon lets spread some cheer,
Better than all the rubbish tweets,
You often see on here.'

****

'*I luv my special twitfam,*
You're always in my heart,
I hate it that I'm poorly,
And it's keeping us apart.
Your tweets mean the world,
And really make me smile,
Here's to all of you,
In proper #harrystyle.'

****

'*Sleeping, sleeping all the time,*
Helps me think of lots of poems and rhymes,
Help Harry Help Others is my campaign,
In aid of all with probs in their brain.'

****

'*I'm gonna keep trying, that's for sure,*
Until one day I find a cure,
Roses are red,
Violets are blue,
My special twitfam, I love you'

****

'I love my twitfam,
You're one of a kind,
When I'm too poorly to tweet,
You're always in my mind.'

****

'Your tweets mean the world,
and really make me smile,
Here's to all of you,
in proper Harry style.'

****

'Sad seeing all these children,
I can't take anymore,
Please support me,
And Help Harry find a cure.'

These, along with his #SMILE, #makeithappen, #PutCANintoCancer and also his yellow smiley faces which would fill the timeline on Twitter just seemed to unite everyone from all walks of life. Harry also loved doing video blogs on a Friday which he would upload onto Twitter so he could update his followers on just how busy he had been during the previous week. He would sometimes sing lines from songs such as the famous James Brown song: 'I feel good…de ne ne ne ne ne…' He was no different on Twitter to the ray of light he was in our own home every single day of the week. I always said he put everyone's lives into perspective.

Another big dream of Harry's was to create 'Harry's Heroes' and to inspire thousands of little 'Harrys' up and down the country. This was going to be the 'big plan' – 'Harry's Heroes' and a 'school's initiative'. He didn't really know the detail behind it, but the basic seeds had been sown by Harry giving his presentation to all those schools. While Harry created everything that he did, it was never about HIM. You see all the different campaigns that are around and the 'bucket lists' people dream up, but Harry was unique. All that was created was by done him, the success of his campaign was down to him and his hard work was all his. He just wanted to raise money for other people because he didn't want anyone else to go through what he was having to endure. To me that just meant that he was going through a horrific ordeal. It hurt Harry to think that others were suffering in the same way as he was and sometimes he would have a cry when he heard about younger children suffering.

Harry loved listening to the radio and especially BRMB radio (now Free Radio) and was invited to go on air with sports presenter Tom Ross. Harry was excited and he just wanted to tell everyone in Birmingham and the West Midlands about his work. He was in good form that day and knew Tom was a staunch Birmingham City supporter, so he arrived donning a bracelet in the colours of their cross-city rivals, Aston Villa. Tom interviewed Harry and asked him about his illness to which Harry replied: 'I have a brain tumour called a Pilocytic Astrocytoma.' Tom was taken aback and said: 'C'mon then, clever clogs. Spell it.' Harry replied instantly: 'I.T.' He was so quick and witty that day and the people in the room fell about in fits of laughter. I loved it when people got to see Harry being quick-witted, as he was like it 24/7 and he was a complete joy to be around. Tom and Harry then talked about the speeches and his achievements and about how confident Harry was. Tom told Harry he would be good on the radio and Harry just replied: 'I am on the radio.' The pair just got on incredibly well and once again, you could see Tom really loved Harry, not because he was ill but because of the sincere boy he was and someone who had achieved just so much for others. Tom absolutely loved his cheeky sense of humour.

A week or so after the website was launched, Harry was back in London, this time for three days. Firstly, on 10th May, Harry was due to deliver a speech on behalf of Cancer Research UK to all their fundraising staff and then, on 13th May, it was the official launch of his campaign. Harry went into school very early on the 10th May to do his SATs, as his head teacher had kindly organised for him to sit them separately to the other children. After he finished the tests, we headed off to London and we arrived in the early afternoon. As soon as we arrived at the hotel, Harry got into his PJ's straight away and went to bed for his usual afternoon 'nap'. Then, during the late afternoon we both set off for Harry to deliver what I considered to be his most important speech to date, a speech to 500 fundraising staff for Cancer Research UK at their annual review. As we arrived at the venue, Harry got up on stage and he appeared so, so tiny in this huge auditorium, but he gave the most exhilarating speech I had ever heard him deliver. He gave his usual speech about himself, his illness, Robert and why he started 'HelpHarryHelpOthers'. Harry also told them the impact that cancer had on us as a family. Harry explained just how important their jobs were to people like him with cancer. He finished off by telling them he had bought them all a bracelet as a gift and that next time they were having a bad day, he hoped they could look at their bracelets and remember just how important their work was to people, like him, who lived in hope of a cure. It goes without saying that there wasn't a dry eye in the house and Harry got a deserved standing ovation. At the end he stood at the doorway to greet everyone as they left the room and, helped by some of the team from Cancer Research UK, he handed out his bracelets.

The next day was also great, as we headed to Hamleys toy store in Regent Street for a bit of fun and a few treats and we also had lunch at the Rainforest Café in nearby Shaftsbury Avenue, which was just like eating in a themed jungle, but in the centre of London. Harry loved it. We always had fun, even if we were doing nothing. He had been to London so many times by now and it was great for him to actually see some of the sights and have a great time.

After an early night it was then 'Harry's day', the day of the official launch of his campaign 'HelpHarryHelpOthers', in partnership with Cancer Research UK. We were staying at the superb Kensington Hotel, supposedly 'London's finest townhouse' and they had kindly put a reception on especially for Harry. Ben Shephard was the host of the launch and Harry couldn't wait to see him again. He had been practising his latest magic trick from a set I had bought him from Hamleys and was looking forward to showing off his new talent in front of Ben. Harry was also excited to be meeting some of his 'special' Twitter friends like TV presenter Wincey Willis and some other special guests like Alison Delaney from Virgin Media, Tania from the Oyster Club, Jo, who was an artist, and another Twitter friend called Brian, who also attended.

It was such a personal day for Harry, too. Besides a few of his Twitter 'friends' some very personal friends attended. These included Robert's widow, Trina, and his colleague and friend, Gaynor. Harry's sister Dani came to London with her friend, too, and it was such a great day. Harry was in his element and Ben opened the event, followed by Harry's speech. He began with: 'Hi, everyone. How you feeling? …Hopefully, like me, with your hands!' He seemed just so well and so happy that day and he delivered another fantastic speech, explaining how excited he was about his partnership with Cancer Research UK. Jools Tait from Cancer Research UK followed Harry and told everyone about their vital work and some facts about brain cancer. Ben Shephard tried to finish off the formalities and thanked everyone for coming: 'Make sure you all grab a bite to eat and mingle and have a chat with Harry's mum, who's looking as lovely as ever today.' Harry then emerged out of nowhere from the audience, marched up to Ben, removed his glasses and said, as he put his own glasses on Ben's face: 'I think you need to borrow these, Ben.' The room just erupted with laughter, Ben included. As Ben looked over at me, laughing, he said: 'She looks even better now, H.' Harry wasn't happy with that and removed the glasses from Ben's head, gave them a clean on his shirt, put them back on Ben's face and said: 'I think you need to go to Specsavers.' Again, that captured Harry's lovable, rogue personality and his very quick-witted nature. He was definitely someone who could get a party started and that memory I will treasure until the day I die.

Following our three exciting and fun days in London, we arrived home on the Thursday and I was told of a big surprise for Harry the following day. One of Harry's friends had arranged for a 'mini launch' of his campaign in Birmingham. They teamed up with Harry's school and sent newsletters out in the community while we were in London. Harry thought he was doing his usual presentation, but the hall was packed and people spilled out into the corridors, which he thought was slightly strange. Following Harry's speech, Tom Ross, James and Oliver Phelps (the Weasley twins from the Harry Potter movies and local Birmingham lads) and ex-footballers Michael Johnson and Ian Taylor burst through the doors and congratulated Harry. It was the first time the Phelps twins, Michael and Ian, had met Harry and they were moved by his work. They could see how amazing Harry was and they all became good friends and stayed in touch with Harry following his presentation that day. It topped a special week for Harry and a week which would start the next chapter for the campaign and for Harry.

The official launch in London with Cancer Research UK was only the beginning for Harry and his campaign was definitely at the next level. He was just thriving and loving life more and more. Just after the launch, another of his special 'Twitfam', a young lady called Kate, had invited Harry into the school where she worked to deliver his 'schools initiative' presentation. Harry immediately came downstairs to tell me: 'Mum, we're going to Darlington.' I thought he had said Darleston (in the West Midlands) as we lived in Birmingham, but oh no, Harry and I were heading to the North East which was the home town of his 'hero' Duncan Bannatyne. Harry even tweeted Duncan excitedly posting a picture of himself on Twitter holding a copy of Duncan's latest book that Harry was going to read on the train. As we were travelling such a long way – I think it was about three hours by train – Harry wanted to 'spread some Harry love', so Kate arranged for him to visit not one but three primary schools whilst he was there. Harry loved seeing children from different towns and telling them all about himself and Robert. He was so pleased to meet Kate and her daughter Ashleigh and just loved the fact that children, even from such a long way away, loved his bracelets and his campaign. He also loved the fact that the school had changed the menu for the day just for Harry and decided to do Harry's favourite meal – a roast dinner with green beans. After presenting at the three schools, it was straight back to the railway station for the three-hour journey home. Harry must have spoken to over eight hundred children that day and it was just brilliant seeing all of them so interested and inspired by Harry.

Another of Harry's special 'Twitfam', a girl called Alison Delaney, invited Harry to speak in front of none other than the CEO of Virgin Media. Once Harry had heard he was to speak in front of the person who reports directly to Sir Richard Branson, he said: 'That's huge.' Most people would be fazed by the thought of speaking to such an influential person, but not Harry. He had this positive 'can do' attitude throughout his life. Once he had decided he was going to go and speak in front of the CEO of Virgin Media, Harry said: 'I can do that.' For someone so young to have such a positive focus on life, I sometimes wonder what his adult life would have been like. So we headed off to the Virgin Media Head Office. Harry loved it because he got to have his first ever ride in the first class section on Virgin Trains and you could see he was just oozing with enthusiasm for the day. Once we arrived in London, he said to himself: 'London. I'm home and I'm here to make it happen.'

When we finally arrived at the Virgin Media offices, Harry got to meet up with Alison Delaney's daughter Robyn, who had also been invited for the day, as she had been inspired by Harry and had made lots of bracelets for 'HelpHarryHelpOthers'. She had introduced Harry's campaign into her school and she headed up the fundraising there, too. As soon as Harry saw Robyn again, he said cheekily: 'Where's Batman?' It was a standing joke between them and just a reminder for everyone to watch what they said, as Harry was very quick off the ball.

Harry was feeling a little tired so he had a bit of a rest and had some refreshments and then he was let into a big room where all the Virgin Media staff were crammed in. They also spilled out of every doorway into the corridors in order to get a view of Harry. The board of directors were also in the room, but Harry wasn't fazed by them one jot. He delivered a polished presentation and, at the end of it, he ensured everyone had a usual laugh at my expense. I always had tears in my eyes seeing Harry delivering his PowerPoint presentations, even though I knew every word that was coming. I was so proud of him and never ever got fed up of listening to him. Harry would always look over at me as soon as he finished as if to say 'I did it mum' and he would see me with tears in my eyes. He then referred back to the two hundred or so people watching and said: 'Oh God, she's blarting again.' Then he went on to remind them that I was not only his mum but his 'bag carrier and chauffeur'. After another great presentation, there were a few questions fired back at Harry and he dealt with them so well and answered them all. He then had a tour of the offices while I spent time with some of the staff at their workstations. Harry was also introduced to 'RED', an imp-like character and the Virgin Media mascot. We were then asked to go into the boardroom with the CEO and we were introduced to the other directors. Harry, as usual, took it all in his stride. I asked Harry if he was OK and he then turned to me and said: 'Mum, I'm OK. You can stay outside.' So, I'd been relegated to standing outside this very plush office, peering in through the glass windows, trying to ensure that Harry was OK! Remember, he was only eleven years old and was sat in the board room with the CEO of Virgin Media and another three or four directors. He looked so calm and was slumped into the chair just like any other little boy would be, at home. I knew Harry wanted feedback from his presentation from the director, as he never got to do his presentation to the 'Dragons', so this was a great opportunity for Harry and I know it meant the world to him, as he wanted to ensure his work was the best it could be. He had to be so word perfect and wanted to ensure they approved. I just stood peering through the window at him in total disbelief. I was thinking to myself: 'Do you know, Harry? You're just brilliant.' I was really proud of him. Harry loved it and he knew it was his time to ask the 'real' businessmen what they thought of his presentation. As it happened, the CEO and directors of Virgin Media were bowled over by Harry; they loved his presentation. The only thing they picked up on was that Harry referred to his notes too many times and they said it would be good if he got to know all of his presentation off by heart. But apart from that, they thought his presentation and the content was excellent and that Harry was an inspirational little boy.

Virgin Media were brilliant towards Harry. They presented him with his own Blackberry phone. He was very proud of his new phone and, if I'm honest, I thought I would get my phone back off Harry, as he always used mine because I didn't think he was old enough to have one of his own. How wrong was I? Harry was very crafty, because the phone that Virgin gave him had a Pay-As-You-Go SIM card, so Harry decided he would still use mum's phone, so that he could use Twitter, as mine was contracted and it wouldn't cost him anything to use – the cheek of him. But that was Harry and I'm so sure he would have been a shrewd businessman one day. Harry loved his special day at Virgin Media and you could see the joy he had by looking at the wonderful photos I had taken of him. I thought that would have been just the start of the next phase for Harry. To be speaking to organisations of that size and to have their complete backing was very special to Harry. Virgin Media also offered to pay for Harry to have a short film made with him telling the story of his campaign sometime in the following weeks.

Sadly, we never got the time to shoot that Virgin Media video because Harry's health deteriorated so quickly after the visit to their offices. Nor did we get the chance for Harry to speak with Sir Richard Branson himself, which the CEO of Virgin Media was going to arrange and Harry was really looking forward to, but we had to cancel the call, due to Harry's health deterioration. He was so proud that Sir Richard wanted to speak to him and I know that he was going to ask him to get behind 'HelpHarryHelpOthers' as he wanted to inspire other children to do good things for whatever they cared about.

I remember another visit to the Kensington Hotel, who had kindly put us up for two days, as Harry had two very important speeches to deliver in town. As we arrived at the hotel, he walked in and said his usual line: 'We're at it again, mum. You don't have to be posh to be privileged, hey?' You could see people glance over at this cheeky little kid in a bright hoody and his tracksuit bottoms. He walked over to reception and just said 'hello' to everyone really confidently. You could see some business people not really sure how to respond and Harry could sense that. You could just tell we were from completely different walks of life, but to Harry it didn't matter. He was just as important as them. He took a little box out of his pocket and looked at the reception staff and the 'well to do' guests and said: 'Wanna see some magic?' By the time Harry had finished showing his magic, you could see the barriers go down and then, when he told them what he was doing in London, delivering speeches to five hundred people, their attitude just completely changed and you could start to feel the warmth from them towards Harry. He was a great icebreaker and I think he knew it.

Everyone and everything else in life was important to Harry; it wasn't just about the celebrities or the big dinners in London; it wasn't just about all the nice venues he was invited to. Harry loved and valued everybody and he loved every event, no matter how big or how small it was. It was always a dream of Harry that when he grew up, he would have a place of his own to stay in when he was in the capital. He once said to me: 'Mum, I'm going to have a 'pad' in London when I grow up.' He loved going to London and I had no doubt, if things had turned out differently, he would have ended up moving to the capital one day. He was very proud of where he was from, but London really engaged in his work and all the events he was invited to or speeches he had to deliver kept bringing him to London. He loved sharing his story and had a 'presence' that only certain people have about them, even though he was only a little boy. He had a certain charm about him that I can't explain and I don't know where he got it from, to be honest. His sense of humour and quick wit enabled him to mingle with adults and just create 'smiles' from everyone he met. Although always looking to tell a joke and make people laugh, there was no arrogance about Harry. He would make a room light up and make your heart melt with his big cheeky smile. Even some of his phrases and facial expressions just made people smile. To Harry, the big events in London were great, but he loved nothing more than being with people and he valued the days he spent selling his bracelets outside the local Asda supermarket, even on cold December mornings and even on Christmas Eve. He would treat everyone the same, whether it was a major celebrity or a waiter serving him a drink, which is the way it really should be. Whatever walk of life we are from and whatever we have or haven't achieved, we are all made of the same. Everyone who is a good, nice person deserves the same respect. Harry understood those values and he always demonstrated them, too, and I made sure of that.

He loved to see his 'regulars' at Asda. There were some lovely old people who would come just to see Harry and they would say: 'Harry, where you been? You haven't been for a while.' Harry loved it and would he would always fill them in on his latest news. He talked to everyone and anyone who passed by, young or old. Harry wasn't just interested in the 'mobile generation' but he also recognised that some people didn't have Twitter or Facebook. But he wanted to let everyone know he was still campaigning. Some people would come to Harry's stand, time and time again, to buy bracelets and have a chat with Harry. If we advertised that Harry would be at a certain location, people would travel from miles away and queue up to see Harry and he really appreciated that.

Shortly after the trip to the Virgin Media offices in the August of 2011 we were invited to a skydiving event in aid of Duncan Bannatyne's Pilgrim Bandits charity at Netheravon, in Wiltshire. The Pilgrims charity helps amputees from the forces and is one of Duncan's favoured charities. He is in fact a patron of it. Harry was kindly invited via a friend of Duncan's on Twitter called Peter Jinks, who later become Harry's good friend, too. I Remember Harry used to Tweet Peter often and once as he knew he was Duncan's friend he was desperate to share a presentation with Peter to get his approval. Harry cared so much about the work he had done himself and remember he was only 11. He was always looking for feedback as he knew the better it could be meant the more it could help. It was a three-hour car journey to get there and Harry really started to become unwell. As soon as we arrived in Wiltshire, he couldn't wait to get out of the car as he had felt sick all the way through the journey. At first, I thought he was suffering from travel sickness, but Harry had been really quiet, all the way down to Wiltshire and he just wasn't himself. Even in the sick state he was, Harry got on with it and went round to meet all the soldiers. He was so touched by their plight that he donated some of his bracelets to the Pilgrims charity. We didn't really spend too much time at the event (or with Duncan) because Harry was just not well enough, so we soon headed back home. We attended the event as Harry had the intention of asking Duncan to become an Ambassador for the campaign, but because of Harry's condition on the day, he didn't get that opportunity. I could see he wasn't himself and I was worried for Harry. Harry still managed to meet some of his beloved Twitfam including Peter Jinks, Lesley and Jonno and I know he was thrilled to be there to support Duncan. It was another of Harry's dreams ticked off even if he wasn't himself and he couldn't stay for as long as he had planned.

5

Why Harry?

*'Harry was bright and intelligent and someone who cared
very much about others.'*
**John Terry (Chelsea and England footballer and an
Ambassador for HHHO)**

I ended up taking Harry to the hospital twice during that particular week in August 2011 following the skydiving event, only for him to be kept in overnight then sent home the next day. But on the second occasion, Harry asked me to take him back to the hospital because he was feeling really bad. When he saw his consultant, they immediately arranged to do a CT scan. The scan showed he had hydrocephalus – a build-up of fluids inside the skull that leads to pressure in the brain – and this was causing the sickness and headaches. The fluid had built up because the tumour had started to grow again and it was causing a blockage, as the fluid had nowhere to drain. Something had to be done and done quickly!

Once the blockage had been discovered, they finally decided to keep Harry in hospital for a week. The doctors wanted to undertake a minor operation to put a 'shunt' in his brain, a bit like a plumbing device which automatically allowed the blocked fluid from the brain to drain out into his body. This would be followed by another operation to remove the tumour. However, when the surgeons looked at his scans in more detail, they decided that they were only going to operate once. They were going to install the 'shunt' at the same time as removing part of the tumour. Both the chemotherapy and radiotherapy had failed and surgery appeared to be the last resort for Harry. Basically, the surgeons told us that if Harry didn't have this surgery, he would die. It was that simple. The surgery would hopefully prolong Harry's life – it was their only option. It was Harry's last chance but we had to wait for a suitable date. For an eleven-year-old child, this was a big deal indeed. It was so hard to grasp, as Harry seemed just so, so well and happy in himself other than suffering from headaches, the usual tiredness and the occasional sickness. The last three years had been relatively calm up to this point, but now it was all about to get rather serious. Suddenly, 'HelpHarryHelpOthers' was on 'hold' and seemingly unimportant to us.

The doctors eventually decided to send Harry home until the date of the surgery came through, even though he was still getting the vile headaches and the doctors prescribed him medicine and tablets (of which he had to take in excess of twenty-four a day to try to control the symptoms). I remember one sunny Sunday afternoon. Harry was sitting in the garden, laughing to himself. Harry always loved poems and every time he'd written a new poem, he would publish it on Twitter. So he had decided to set up something called 'TwitPoemFestSunday'. As soon as he had got this up and running, he was bombarded with funny little poems sent by his Twitter 'friends' and as he sat there reading them, he just burst out into fits of laughter. In between all this laughter, he would have a nap on the sun lounger with his blanket over him. Generally, he seemed in good spirits at that time but in reality he was really very ill.

Once Harry knew he faced brain surgery, rather than dwelling on his situation, he actually saw it as an opportunity to expand his campaign and thought it would be an even better campaign because he could soon tell people that he had had every treatment to do with brain cancer – chemotherapy, radiotherapy and soon the surgery to remove part of the tumour and to install the 'shunt'. He thought he could tell everyone about his experiences. For an eleven-year-old boy, that type of outlook is remarkable, in my view. He didn't realise at the time how many people he actually impacted on, all over the world, just by 'chatting' on Twitter or by meeting people personally at special events. He had this amazing gift for listening to people. He would listen to anybody, really, and would give anyone his time. He had all those followers on Twitter because he spent the time replying to as many people as possible. He wanted to tell all of them that he cared and that every one of them was important. Harry met a lot of celebrities, but to him every individual, regardless of what walk of life or background they were from, was important to him. For such a young boy, Harry had some amazing qualities. In my eyes, there are no more special gifts or qualities than sharing your time or listening to others. Harry was just there for everyone and although he was fortunate enough to go to some amazing places and meet some incredible people, he was very grounded and more special than anyone will ever realise. However, as the afternoon on that Sunday moved into late evening, his health began to deteriorate, his headaches returned and he started to get stressed, so we rushed him back to the hospital as a precaution. We took him to the A & E department where the doctors examined Harry and decided that he was in a critical condition and they had to do the surgery as soon as possible. However, Harry had eaten that day so the surgery had to wait until the next day. So they kept him in overnight and we were told that Harry was on the emergency list for the next morning. I feared for Harry, because the operation to insert a 'shunt' was a very delicate one and it could easily go wrong. I was warned that 'shunts' could block easily and sometimes people could have a lot of problems with them at first. However, I couldn't stand seeing the headaches getting Harry down and preventing him doing the things he wanted to do and finally, after lots of persistence, something was at last going to be done about them. I just prayed that the 'shunt' operation would go smoothly and Harry would instantly feel better in his head. I just wanted to cuddle him and I so wished I could make him better, but the worse thing was I was powerless and Harry's life was in the hands of those marvellous surgeons and in the hands of God.

The plan was to undertake one operation to remove part of the tumour and install the 'shunt' but due to the seriousness of Harry's condition the doctors decided to just install the 'shunt'. That had now been 'fast-tracked', as his health was in a serious condition. Following the surgery to install the 'shunt', which lasted two hours, Harry's headaches had disappeared and he seemed to be beginning his road to recovery. A few days after the operation, he said he was feeling a lot better. We thought he would be sent home not long after the surgery and then sit and wait for the next scan in a month's time. However, just before Harry was discharged, I had noticed he was sleeping more and I mentioned this to one of the nurses at the time. She had already done some checks on his eyes and noticed his pupils were very sluggish, which was an indication something wasn't right. It was then that I knew this wasn't going to be an easy ride for Harry. The doctors did some more thorough checks on Harry and they proved his sodium levels were very low. Sometimes if your salt levels are very low, you can go into a coma and this explained why Harry was very sleepy. The doctors decided that it would be too risky for Harry to go home, so they insisted he should be kept in under observation. Harry had been in hospital for a week already and all he wanted to do was to go home before he faced his next big surgery to remove some of the tumour.

Harry didn't understand why he had become unwell so quickly because, while he was awake, he was his normal bubbly self but for most of the time following his surgery, he was asleep. However, he didn't look that unwell. Some people who have cancer tend to deteriorate rapidly and you can see they're ill, but we didn't have that with Harry. His headaches had gone, too, and we were beginning to think he was showing signs of recovery at last. He even said to me that he had things to do at home and wanted to continue his campaign, even though his tumour was still growing and it was making him more and more tired as each day passed. Harry was in no fit state to work on his campaign, but as he was such a determined lad, he thought he was letting everyone down by being in hospital. He was sleeping almost twenty hours a day and when we woke him up so he could have something to eat, he would go back to sleep as soon as he had finished eating, saying something like: 'Mum, I'm going to do what I do best. I'm going back to sleep.' For those three or four hours when he was awake, though, he was simply 'Harry'.

We had planned to take Harry on holiday before he faced the biggest challenge of his life, but with his condition so severe, we decided the only thing to do was to cancel those plans, as he wasn't allowed home. The best we could do was to take him outside into the hospital grounds in his wheelchair, just to give him some fresh air and a change of scenery.

Harry also entertained not only himself but the nurses, too, by writing or shouting out poems across the ward. I remember one Sunday afternoon, when the ward was quite empty, as some of the children had gone home for the weekend. Harry was sat up in bed and we were all thinking of objects or topics like 'chair', for example, and we would all have to make up a short poem about that object or topic. One of the nurses working that day was called Patrick. Harry got on with really well with Patrick and he was the topic on one occasion. Immediately, Harry shouted across the ward to Patrick, who was at the nursing station, that he had a poem for him:

> *'Patrick, Patrick, he looks after me,*
> *He does lots of things,*
> *and he even measures my wee.'*

Harry sat there, chuckling his head off and he knew he was very funny. He was fascinated that the nurses had to measure his urine, so it tended to be a big topic of conversation (or poem in this case). He helped me keep my spirits up during those dark days in the hospital and I just loved every minute of every day with him, even though he was seriously ill.

Harry was very popular and had lots of visitors in hospital; obviously close family and friends, but also some famous friends who had heard Harry speak or had met him at various events Harry had attended in the past. Harry had made such an impact on these people when he did speeches or presentations and they kindly stayed in touch with our little boy. Among his famous visitors were Harry's favourite 'Dragon', Duncan

Bannatyne, local radio presenter, Tom Ross, Aston Villa legend Ian Taylor, ex-Birmingham City defender, Michael Johnson, TV presenter Wincey Willis and James and Oliver Phelps from the Harry Potter movies. As an average family we were completely blown away that these famous people would all come and spend time with Harry in hospital. It was all rather humbling actually to think that Harry had made such an impact on so many people's lives, including people who were well-known and famous and led very busy and successful lives themselves.

For the first time in nearly four years, there was a real possibility that, if the surgery to remove part of the tumour went well, Harry's tumour would be the smallest it had ever been. It was our only real hope for Harry and maybe we saw it as a formality that the surgery would be successful and, more importantly, it would buy time for Harry. The morning of the surgery soon rolled around and Harry had received tons of 'Get Well' cards and messages from people all over the country. He appeared to be OK in himself; he was happy and giggling as we were trying to get on his surgical stockings in preparation for his surgery. When the anaesthetist appeared, about ten minutes prior to Harry going into theatre, he asked: 'Harry, are you allergic to anything?' to which Harry duly replied with his quick, dry wit: 'Err, yes …Hospitals and girls.' We all erupted into fits of laughter, including the anaesthetist, and it lightened the mood a little. Harry was all gowned up but he still insisted on sending a Tweet out to his 'Twitfam', only minutes before he faced surgery. I can't remember the exact words on the Tweet (and it's still too raw to look over and read Harry's Tweets) but it was something along the lines of: 'Going down for my op now. Don't worry about me. I'm just gonna have a big sleep. When I'm back I'll be better. I love you all.' He also enclosed a picture of himself in the gown, giving them all a big wave. He was so fond of his true 'Twitfam' and they were always in his heart. I had my strict instructions to keep them updated and I wasn't going to let him down.

I felt physically sick inside and, as we walked Harry down to theatre, I just said in my head over and over again: 'Please look after him. Please, God, keep him safe.' By now, Harry was getting a little scared. I don't know whether it was a premonition or something, but Harry told me just before he'd been anaesthetised that he'd had a nightmare a few months before that he was going to die during surgery. I quickly reassured him by reminding him of all the children that he had seen go down to have brain surgery over the three weeks he had been in hospital and not one of them had faced any complications. I hugged him so tightly and promised him I would be right by his side every single minute until he woke up. We all kissed him, told him how much we loved him and said that we'd see him when he woke up. As he fell asleep through the anaesthetic, my emotions all came out and I begged the surgeons to take good care of him. Then I broke down in tears.

We all walked outside for what seemed like the longest day of our lives. Harry's surgery was anticipated to last around five and a half hours, but even knowing this I couldn't leave the hospital just to pass the time away. I had to be very close to Harry, just in case anything happened to my boy. Being apart from Harry was the hardest thing to do and Darren and I also had to remain positive in front of his brother and sister. We all knew that there would be a risk that the surgery could leave Harry blind or he could lose the movement in the left side of his body. Our biggest fear was for him to lose his sight. Harry was such a bright, happy, bubbly person and after having eleven years of vision, even though he wore glasses, I couldn't bear the thought of him being in sudden darkness. But whatever Harry faced, I had no doubt we would all face it as a family and he would still receive the best possible care, love and attention that he could have asked for.

We were all pacing up and down the floor in the area that Harry was due to return to on the Neurosurgery Ward, waiting expectantly for any news from the doctors. Harry had gone down to surgery at 9am, so when 3pm came we just thought: 'Any minute now our beautiful boy will be returned to us, asleep but safe and sound.' 3pm came and went and so did 4pm, 5pm and 6pm, just as quickly, and we began to worry for Harry. But then we thought that, hopefully, it was only a sign that they were removing more of his tumour. Darren and I kept walking towards the theatre doors waiting anxiously for any sign of movement. Suddenly, one of the neurosurgery team appeared and said that the surgery was over, but during the operation Harry had suffered a haemorrhage, as they'd cut through one of his blood vessels, due to the awkward location of the tumour. They had rectified the haemorrhage but, as Harry had been through such a major operation, they were transferring him straight to the Intensive Care Unit (ICU) to 'give his body a rest', as they described it. We were then told that they were putting him on a ventilator and were going to sedate him to give him a complete rest. We waited in anticipation to see him, but we were relieved it was all over for Harry. Even then I thought: 'How can this be?' I also thought: 'Why? Why? Why? Why Harry?'

Although I couldn't believe Harry was in ICU, I was so relieved to see my beautiful boy and I just wanted to hold him tightly, but he was on a life support machine. I just broke down in tears again at the sight of him lying there, motionless. It just wasn't right. I'd have done anything to swap places with him, but I just kept thinking: 'At least he's having the rest he deserved after going through nine hours of surgery.' To be honest, I was just in complete shock, disbelief and I desperately wanted to cuddle Harry, but I couldn't. He had wires and tubes coming out of both hands and every part of his body and he had a bandage all round his little head, which I expected, as the surgery was done right across the top of his head. I wasn't able to kiss his lips or stroke his head as I always used to do. The pain I felt inside was just unbearable. To see your little boy like this is something you just don't imagine and shouldn't have to witness as a parent. I kept thinking of all the children we had seen go through similar surgery and how they had gone back onto the ward straight afterwards and I just couldn't understand why this had happened to our baby boy. To see how upset his brother and sister were was too much and it hurt us to see them suffering as well. No child should see that at their age, but it was their choice to be there, close to their brother. They were all so close and it wouldn't have been right for them not to have seen Harry.

I had to remain positive for the children's sakes and I reassured them by saying: 'At least he's getting one-to-one care in here and he won't know anything about it. He's just having a big sleep and, when he's had a big enough rest, we will be here when he wakes up'. The hospital kindly offered me the parents' accommodation but there was no way I was going to leave Harry's side. I hadn't left his bedside in the three weeks leading up to the operation and there was no way I was about to leave him now, in his hour of need. I asked for a chair and I stayed by his side. That's all I needed at that time. I spent the time talking to him and touching him even though he probably couldn't hear me and didn't know I was there, as he had been heavily sedated.

After 48 hours Harry was still sedated but his ventilator had been reduced and he began breathing by himself. It was a relief to see the ventilator had been taken away and to see his beautiful rosebud lips again. We were then told by the doctor that they were going to stop his sedation, so I immediately thought he'd be awake very soon, within hours. Darren and I just sat there, watched and waited for him to wake up, talked to him and constantly told him we loved him. Harry was still asleep overnight and, come the following morning, he was finally transferred out of ICU. It was the biggest relief ever but, worryingly, he was still in a coma. The huge overwhelming relief of seeing him back on the ward was just the tonic we needed, though. It seemed like it could only be an upwards journey for Harry from now on – surely?

Three days after Harry had gone back onto the ward and into the High Dependency Unit (HDU) area, he was still asleep but he was definitely aware of what was going on. If we asked him for a thumbs-up or a squeeze of the hand, he would respond to our request. I remember that when I asked Harry to pucker his lips, he didn't disappoint. Even though Harry was still in a coma we remained optimistic throughout and the doctors reassured us that it was 'just a matter of time'. Every morning, I used to wake up thinking it was the day that Harry was also going to wake up. Each day was full of excitement and great hope – you have to live in hope otherwise you may as well give up. Unfortunately, by the end of each day we were downhearted. We desperately wanted our Harry back, as I missed him so very much. We were always inseparable and always chatted, loved, laughed, sang and just did everything together and seeing him asleep like this was killing me; it was killing us as a family. It was already feeling like a very lonely world without him being awake.

One week had passed by and Harry was still asleep. By this stage we were so concerned for Harry but the doctors kept reassuring us that he would wake up in his own time. However, I suddenly noticed that Harry had stopped responding to our requests. He had stopped squeezing our hands and was no longer blowing kisses like he had been for the previous few days. I knew that there was something wrong and that Harry was deteriorating, for whatever reason. We kept telling the doctors of our concerns and they constantly scanned him and checked the pressure of his 'shunt'. We were told that the pressure can sometimes slow down and the 'shunt' can become blocked, following any subsequent surgery, just as we had been advised before the operation. However, the doctors assured us that there was no issue with the 'shunt'. I felt like I was going mad and there was absolutely nothing I could do to help Harry's situation but to wait and wait and that is what hurt so much.

Three whole weeks had passed and Harry was due to have his first MRI scan following his surgery. That would hopefully tell us more about the operation and if it had been successful or not. Some of the swelling which had been caused by the operation should have reduced by that time and the scan should have given the doctors some indication if things were as they should be. The morning after the scan, Darren and I waited at the hospital anxiously for the doctors to explain the results. We saw the morning registrars doing their rounds and they appeared nervous as they approached Harry's bedside, but the news they gave us suggested that the scan appeared to be OK. Darren asked a lot of questions and the doctors answered them as best as they could, but overall they seemed pleased with progress and again it was 'just a matter of time' before we would see any real change in his condition. Relief and contentment can't begin to describe our feelings at the time; relief that there didn't appear to be anything wrong with the scan results. The relief turned to concern, though, about four hours later, when Harry's neurosurgeon asked to speak to us while we were at Harry's bedside and wanted to know how we thought Harry was doing. I explained that I was concerned, as Harry wasn't responding in the way he was before the operation and he replied that he was also concerned. I looked at Darren in astonishment and turned to the surgeon and asked: 'What do you mean? The doctors this morning said everything looked OK with the scan results.' His reply was: 'Well, I've looked at the scan and although at least fifty per cent of the tumour has been removed, it appears to be bigger than it was before the surgery.' I just couldn't take in the information the surgeon was giving us. How was this possible? We had been on a bit of a 'high' all morning, thinking everything was as it should be but now, 'bang', we were once again thrown into a sense of shock, despair and total disbelief by what the neurosurgeon was telling us. Surely there was some mistake; he had to be wrong. We asked the surgeon what it meant for Harry. Would they have to operate again? He replied by saying that, due to Harry still being in a coma and due to him haemorrhaging during the operation, further surgery wasn't an option at that stage, as there would be too much of a risk to Harry. He was due to speak to Harry's oncologist later that day, to decide what action to take next. Again, all we could do was to sit and wait. It was at that stage that I really feared for Harry and I was full of all sorts of emotions: anger, upset, heartache. You name it, I felt it. I just wanted my son back with me. I wanted to know what had happened to him. It was all too much to comprehend. It felt like we were going one step forward and three steps back. Why couldn't God shine down on him and look after him? Harry had done so much for others and I just felt the world was closing in on me. Life can be so cruel, sometimes. Why is that? I don't suppose anyone will ever know the answer?

Harry's oncologist was a great man. I always felt comforted when I saw him and I had every faith in him. He listened and he knew Harry and I knew he wouldn't give up and would always fight for Harry's corner. Chemotherapy appeared to be the only option left for Harry, but they were going to administer it orally, fed through by Nasogastric Intubation (an NG tube) as he couldn't have the intensive chemo he'd had before, due to him being in a coma. The Oncologist explained that the type of chemo, which was called Vincristine, would target the blood vessels feeding the tumour and causing it to grow. Again, we went through all the emotions in the book, but as long as we had hope we wouldn't give up on Harry. I would never have given up on Harry. I just wanted the treatment to start immediately, so that the tumour would stop growing. It was already taking over Harry and we knew that this was the reason why he was still in a coma. We needed more time to let the chemo work and kick in, so that the tumour would start to reduce in size and Harry would eventually wake up.

After a further seven weeks Harry was still going through his chemotherapy treatment and there was still no change. Harry remained in a coma. It felt like we were living a bad dream. It was such an emotional rollercoaster ride – watching, waiting, hoping – but I didn't care that much, if it just meant Harry would eventually recover and wake up. We then started noticing that Harry was giving out a groaning sound and had begun moving his left arm. He looked in some discomfort. One day, he managed to pull up his arm, groaned and then cried. I immediately told the doctors and nurses about the movements and the registrar promised he would keep an eye on him. He had no idea what was going on with Harry and why he was making those noises and movements. By this time, I was very angry and so concerned and all I wanted to know was what was wrong with my Harry. That particular day was meant to be a very special day for Harry as his 'hero', Duncan Bannatyne, paid an unplanned visit especially to see Harry. He had come to the hospital in Birmingham on his own and he just sat with Harry, holding his hand and talked to him for about two and half hours, telling him he had to get better because he wanted to take Harry for a swim at his villa. It was quite an amazing day and I am sure Harry knew Duncan was there by his side because even though Harry was still in a coma, he had his left eye ajar while Duncan was talking to him and tilted his head slightly towards Duncan when he spoke to Harry. Little did I know that this would be the last time that Harry would make any movement for days following Duncan's visit. The doctors still didn't know why Harry had made these groans and movements but whatever it was it had made Harry stop moving completely. For several weeks before, even though Harry didn't respond to our requests, he would make slight voluntary movements like a little scratch here or there, but now he wasn't even doing that.

A few days later, Harry finally had a CT (Computed Tomography) scan and I knew immediately that it wasn't good news, because the doctors wanted to see us at a specific time. It was normal for Harry's consultant to see us, but this time he was accompanied by a neurosurgeon who was also one of the registrar team that had seen Harry almost every day since the surgery. As we went into the meeting room, they revealed that Harry now had a thrombosis in the vessels of the brain and it had moved down into his jugular. Although it seemed like everything was stacking up against Harry, I refused to give up on him and I sure wasn't going to let anyone else give up either, even though I understood the seriousness of what the doctors were saying. We were told that Harry would have to have a stronger dose of medicine called Klexane, an anticoagulant which thins the blood. During that evening, Harry's breathing began to deteriorate and by the following morning, the ICU team were back round his bed and he was given full oxygen, but even that wasn't enough. As a precaution, Harry had to go back to ICU, where he was sedated and put on a ventilator again. Anger began to build up within me and if I'd heard the words 'his body needs a rest' or 'it is just a matter of time' once more, I think I would have throttled someone. For the first time for quite a while, I just lost it and completely broke down as we followed Harry and the doctors back to ICU. It was so heart-breaking. I couldn't believe what was happening to Harry. As I've said before, he appeared to be so well before the surgery, but now it didn't look good, as he was back in ICU and it was all too much to take in and we didn't have time for any of it to sink in, because it was all happening too fast. We just had to get on with it and be there for Harry's sake.

After what seemed like a lifetime but was actually about a week in ICU, Harry once again started to breathe for himself, but the doctors decided to keep the ventilator in. He was in a cubicle on his own, due to him being on chemo, although the doctors decided to postpone this while he was in ICU. Harry's consultant decided to get the Neurologist to take a look at Harry and he arranged for an EEG scan (electroencephalogram). I had no idea what news would come from that scan, but I knew that it would measure Harry's brain activity. On the same day as the EEG scan, Duncan just happened to be in the hospital again, as he was opening a new ward there. Once again he found time to visit Harry in ICU and sat there holding his hand.

Then, one of the doctors from the ICU came into see me and asked me to come outside the unit for a chat. I liked her approach and appreciated her honesty as she explained what was happening to Harry, rather than talking down to me. However, the news she was telling me wasn't what I wanted to hear and from the moment she started to speak, the look in her eyes told me that it was 'last chance saloon' for Harry. The doctor revealed that Harry had very slow and abnormal brain activity and if there was the slightest chance the brain could recover, then they were going to test it by giving Harry Class A drugs. She warned us that they were going to start administering the drugs immediately. Her tone was direct, but it wasn't meant in a nasty way – more the fact that she wanted me to understand that Harry had to continually improve over the next three to five days, because it was his last chance to survive. The news threw me back even more. How can any parent comprehend the news that their child has one last chance to stay alive? I guess I knew that this kind of news is repeated every day of the week in every town in the world, but it was happening to me; It was happening to my family. I felt defeated and crushed on hearing the news and I still couldn't believe it, as no one could tear me and Harry apart; no one could tear the family apart. We were all so close and Harry and I were a team. This just had to work.

Our eyes were glued on Harry as soon as the drugs were administered. I could see his left eye was slightly open at first but it soon closed when the drugs kicked in. Overnight there was no change in Harry's condition and it was the same the following day. It was not looking good for Harry, and Darren and I knew what was about to happen. On day three, we had a big meeting with the doctors and they confirmed there was nothing else they could do for Harry. There was no chance his brain would recover and there was little hope of him waking up from his coma. As soon as we had received the dreaded news, plans were put in place to send Harry home to spend his final days where he belonged. Harry was such a homely boy and all he had ever wanted before the surgery was to go home and I'd assured him that would happen. All of a sudden there were doctors and nurses rushing around everywhere, making the plans happen. We were to go home with Harry on Friday 7th October at 8am.

On the Thursday evening, the night before we were to take Harry home, we were all around his bed, talking to him just like we always did. While I was talking to him, I noticed his head turn towards me and then it turned back, so I asked him to do it again but he didn't. When I look back I think that was when Harry actually 'left' us. It was his way of saying 'goodbye' in the best way he could; in the only way he could. I thought I'd had lots of 'worst days of my life' but that night surely topped them all. I couldn't believe that the following morning I would be taking my little soul mate and hero home to die. It was just so very wrong and it wasn't meant to be like that. Children are supposed to outlive their parents; not the other way round.

That last night in the hospital seemed to go so quickly and all I wanted to do was to cradle Harry and get into bed with him, but I had to settle for just holding his hand and stroking his head. I just sat there watching him and none of it seemed to sink in. How could I ever come to terms with the fact that my child was going to die? How could any parent cope with that feeling? I just couldn't cope with it and, to this day, I still can't get my head round it. I don't think I ever will. Maybe I won't want to. Even after what had been said, I refused to give up and the hope was there that Harry would prove everyone wrong. I prayed throughout the night in the hope that his condition would improve, but the reality was quite the opposite. He'd had enough and, by the morning, he was back on full ventilation again and the doctors were extremely concerned: so much so, they tried to get the ambulance rearranged for an earlier time, to transport Harry home as soon as they could.

I stood outside his room in ICU peering through the window at what appeared to be something like a military operation for the ambulance crew and the doctors to prepare him for his last journey home and, throughout this time, Harry had to remain on his mobile ventilator. As we left ICU and walked down the corridors I just couldn't take it all in. How could I be taking Harry home to die? It didn't make sense. None of it made sense and it felt like my world was about to end. He was just so well only a few months before and he was my best friend. How could I accept he was going to die? I couldn't accept it and I never will, but I have to live with it. I sat in the ambulance with him and just kept telling him we were going home. I knew Harry would have wanted that. I couldn't let him pass away in hospital. Home was so important to him and although we didn't have long, I wanted his last moments to be with the five of us. My head was all over the place and I felt like I was going through a never ending dark tunnel and that I'd never be able to find my life again. I just couldn't comprehend what life would be like without Harry and what it would be like for the family. There would only be four of us now. I was so upset and angry with the world and everyone around me and still, to this day, I just don't get it. I kept thinking of those last moments we had with Harry before his surgery (all those weeks ago in August) and those cuddles and love we shared proved to be the last real time we had with Harry. The minute we kissed him goodbye before going into surgery on 10th August 2011 was the day he was really taken away from us. I was so angry that we never got him back for a spilt second and it was hard to take in that we didn't even have a day with him when he was fully awake. That was the day we lost Harry forever and in his place would be a lifetime of pain, emptiness and the biggest void ever.

As we arrived home, his 'special' bed was waiting for him in the lounge and we had to leave for a few moments so that the doctors could remove his ventilator. They hung around for an hour or so as they thought he would go quite quickly, but only I knew that Harry would have wanted one last night at home and that's exactly what he had. His breathing became quite bad on the Friday but he stayed with us overnight. I hoped he knew we were all there loving him and talking to him – I'm sure he did. I lowered his bed really low and dropped the rails. I put my sofa next to him so it become like a double bed. We all curled up with Harry. Louie lay at the bottom of his bed and Dani and I at the side of him and Darren stayed downstairs, too. I lay there talking to him all night and loved him just like we did when he used to sneak into my bed when he was younger. I will always be eternally grateful to the amazing team of doctors and nurses who helped us bring Harry home to spend one last night with us.

I always said that everyone needs a 'Harry' in their life. Why was God about to take ours away from us? Life just doesn't seem fair and I will never understand that. Harry had never hurt anyone and had done so much wonderful work to help others who were suffering like he was. If anyone deserved to be here on earth, it was Harry.

6

Falling into the Arms of Angels

'His wit was something that is very hard to come by. For us, he was a very special guy to meet and his message, above everything else, was to be happy, which we could all learn from.'
Oliver Phelps (who played George Weasley in the Harry Potter movies and is an Ambassador for HHHO)

Harry fell asleep in my arms at home at 11.10pm on Saturday 8th October 2011. There were just the five of us in the house at the time: Harry, me, Darren, and Harry's brother and sister, Louie and Danielle. It was just the hardest thing to contemplate that we wouldn't be able to speak to, touch or love Harry again. I had always hoped he would make a recovery and he would prove all the doctors wrong, but maybe that was wishful thinking. On that day, though, it was different and right up to the time he passed away, I knew the end was near for Harry. His breathing had become shallower and I sensed that, at any minute, he would fall asleep forever into the arms of the angels. I had always promised Harry that I would be there for him and I was there right until the very end, holding him tightly in my arms, reassuring him that whatever happened, he would be OK. I was desperate for him to know that he wasn't alone. I felt like I'd let him down big time, because when he went down to theatre for his surgery I'd promised him he'd be OK. How wrong was I?

Although Harry had passed away, to me, as Harry's mum, it felt like I'd still very much got Harry with me. Dead or alive, he was still my beautiful baby, who looked like he was going to wake up at any minute. But the coldness of his body reminded me that the reality was a totally different story. After four long, exhausting months of highs and lows and spending twenty-four hours a day, seven days a week in hospital at Harry's side, we knew that the two long weeks leading up to his funeral on 20th October would be our last time spent with Harry forever. I think that the time between the death of a close loved one and their funeral is probably the hardest and longest period in your life. It was so difficult to explain to people (and still is), but I felt very much like I still had Harry with me, even though he wasn't there in a physical sense. It was so hard to take in what had happened and I struggled to understand that Harry had gone forever. Why had it all happened so quickly? Why wouldn't we be able to see Harry's smiling face again or be able to hear his laughter again? Why couldn't we hug him, love him or touch him again? How could he just go, without saying 'goodbye'? How could my son be snatched from our lives so easily? He was only eleven years old - it was no age. I just didn't get it! I will never ever understand. The feeling of total devastation rushed through me. Anyone who knew me and Harry understood how very close we were. We were an inseparable team and now that team had been broken apart.

Harry remained in the house with us until the Sunday morning and I lay with him all night, telling him how brave he had been and how I loved him so much. When they came to collect his body to take him to Acorns Hospice in Selly Oak, Birmingham, where he would stay until the day before the funeral, I felt such despair. I'd never been separated from Harry – never – but suddenly it had been taken out of my control and he was about to be taken away from me for ever. None of it made sense. It was too much to take in, because only five days before Harry's passing, it was 'still down to time' for Harry (as the doctors kept telling me) and we were still longing for him to wake up and hoping for him to make a recovery. Then we were told 'that was it' and there was no longer any hope for Harry. The news was just so shocking, but there had been no time to grieve, as we only had a couple of days to prepare to bring Harry home to die. This was the cruel reality of how brain cancer can dramatically change and take hold of people's lives.

As a parent, you should never have to face losing your child so young and, although Harry had been ill for four years, at the end he was taken in such a quick and tragic way. It was just the most dreadful and painful feeling and I don't think it will ever leave me. It genuinely felt like I had lost Harry to a tragic accident rather than a serious and life-threatening disease like brain cancer. I'd honestly always feared the worst ever since Harry's diagnosis, but he'd seemed so well in himself, with three years of continuous MRI scans showing all was stable. We never lost hope, right up to the very end. Just one week before Harry was admitted to hospital to undergo surgery, he'd been in front of the CEO of Virgin Media, delivering one of his PowerPoint presentations. What happened to Harry was so sudden and it wasn't the 'norm' that you would expect from someone losing their fight to cancer.

I didn't want to carry on with my life, but I knew I had to face life without Harry and that was the hardest thing for me to comprehend. I knew that once we had set the date for the funeral, it would be like a ticking clock counting down and I had to come to terms with what had happened and I'd never ever be able to share the good times with Harry again after that date. We all spent as much time as possible with Harry at Acorns in the 'special bedroom' which was a children' bedroom, decorated in Harry's favourite SpongeBob character wallpaper. However, it was so cold in there. That didn't matter to us though, as we wrapped up and got used to the temperature and were just glad we could still be with Harry and have the time to say 'goodbye' to him properly. With spending so much time as we could with Harry and planning his funeral, the little time we had to ourselves was spent at home and it was our time to reflect on the four years since Harry had been diagnosed with that dreadful disease. We just kept asking: 'Why Harry? Why us? For all he had done for others, why has such a selfless and innocent young boy been taken away from us?' Unfortunately, no one had the answer and no one ever will.

Suddenly, we had calm and quiet for the first time in our lives. But that wasn't necessarily a good thing – it was just wrong and I didn't like it! It was a really horrible place to be and I think our home will always be like that. We didn't realise until after Harry's passing just how much of an impact he had on people's lives; on our lives. It was only after we started to plough through the hundreds of sympathy cards and the messages on his Twitter account, which Harry adored, that we realised how popular Harry actually was, not just in the UK but globally. We were bombarded with messages. There seemed to be a message popping up every second saying how sorry they were about Harry's passing. Even people we hadn't ever met before or hadn't heard of were contacting us and we didn't mind at all, as each and every one of the messages we received were written from the heart and we appreciated the time people took to write to us about the impact Harry had made on their lives, however small or large it was. We also received hundreds of beautiful letters from people who just wished us well as a family. We were all blown away with all the kindness and just thought: 'Wow …Harry was just our little boy but he was in the thoughts of tens of thousands of people every day.'

Harry was always 'special' and we knew that, from day one, but none of us knew (and indeed Harry didn't know) the love out there for him. We simply didn't know how he had reached out, touched and inspired so many people around the world. His death had an impact on thousands (if not millions) of people around the globe, yet he was just an eleven-year-old boy from a working class Midlands family.

I'd always told Harry I would have done anything to swap places with him and I would often say something like: 'Harry, you know I'd swap heads with you, if I could and give you my brain?' Harry, true to form, would reply: 'Err, no thanks, mum. Have you seen your head? My brain may be poorly, but at least I have one.' He always made light of the darkest of situations, but now that shining light had faded for good and it meant our world would always be in darkness with the loss of Harry.

It was twelve days from the day Harry departed this world until the day of his funeral on 20th October 2011. The time just seemed to go so quickly and all we wanted to do was to be with Harry at Acorns, but we had a funeral to organise. I had never planned a funeral in my life and, quite frankly, I didn't know where to start, though I knew it would be a rather 'special' funeral for a 'special' little boy. Initially, I thought to myself: 'How can I plan the funeral for my baby?' It was not real and it was all so very wrong, but in circumstances like these, you seem to have an inner strength that you just don't know where it comes from. When we weren't at Acorns, spending our final days with Harry, we had no time at all to think about how we really felt, both mentally and physically, as we were just so focussed on arranging Harry's funeral. He had to have the very best send-off ever and we had only a few days to 'make it happen' for Harry. It just had to be a funeral to reflect the bright, colourful, cheery, loving and caring person that he was. I never wanted Harry to be in darkness and, as it was 'his day', I kept telling myself: 'I've the rest of my life to deal with the pain and the grief I feel right now, but I have to hold it together for Harry.' Nothing seemed good enough for my beautiful boy, but we tried to choose what we thought Harry would have wanted, had he ever planned his own funeral. It had to be the brightest and most colourful of days (as far as a funeral could ever be), but at the same time it had to be tasteful. Inside, I was in a dark place, sitting there talking to the funeral directors, who were just doing their job, to be fair. To them, it was 'just another funeral' I guess, but to us, it was going to be our darkest day. Then there were the church ministers, who wanted to know what songs were to be played and the order of the service – all very routine stuff but essential detail. I was still in total disbelief that I could be doing this at all.

We decided on a 'SpongeBob' theme for the funeral; it was Harry's favourite TV programme after all. It kept it bright and childlike and we insisted on the men being dressed in yellow ties in order to brighten up their black suits. Harry loved animals, so we chose a horse-drawn carriage to take Harry on his final journey, rather than the routine hearse. It was to be a spectacular day and just what Harry deserved, but a day I didn't want to happen. What parent would? It was all coming together, apart from the speech. I would sit in the special room at Acorns in total silence, watching over Harry for hours, but the more I thought about what I wanted to say at the service, the more the words just wouldn't come. No words were good enough to describe Harry and I found it hard, as I just couldn't comprehend what had happened and had no idea what to write about.

The days were counting down and it was soon time for Harry to come home for the final time. This would be the last time we would ever spend with him as a family and be able to touch and hold our beautiful, special boy. Harry was such a homely boy and when he wasn't at school, in hospital or doing his endless campaign work, he would be at home, sitting in front of the TV in his pyjamas with us and that's how it had to be for one last time. The private ambulance pulled up outside our house at around 2.30pm on the day before the funeral and we went to escort Harry into the house. It was so hard to see him come out of the ambulance in a coffin, which was covered in a Union Jack sheet. For the last eleven or so days, Harry had laid in his special bedroom at Acorns in a normal bed, but now he would spend his last day at home in a coffin. I felt physically sick at the sight, as I escorted his coffin into our house. Once in the house, we had him placed in the centre of the lounge because he was always at the hub of our home. We all sat with him and put the cartoon channel on the TV, even though no one really wanted to watch it. I couldn't leave his side, so I stayed up all night with him and continued to put some words together for the reading. I had to get the words right, but I was running out of time and I was tired. Eventually though, the words came, but I still think to this day that there will never be enough words to describe my undying love and feelings for Harry.

Harry was dressed in his pyjamas and his favourite hoody with 'happy colours' (as he called them) on the hood. His favourite SpongeBob blanket was wrapped around him and there was a photo of the five of us together, along with a selection of his favourite teddies inside the coffin with him. There was also his favourite picture of himself with the 'Dragons' when they presented him with an award at the Grosvenor Hotel. That was Harry's proudest moment of his short life, but he'd had so many moments to be proud of for someone so young.

The morning of the 20th October – the day of the funeral – quickly came around after a long night spent writing my speech and staring at Harry's coffin. All I could think about was the dread of the funeral directors arriving at the house to put the lid on Harry's coffin, then removing Harry from our house for the last time. I felt such an indescribable pain from that moment and, to this day, I can still feel it and always will. It was like a huge heavy weight had been placed in my head, in my heart and in my stomach, all at the same time. I know that pain will never lessen, although people tell me it will 'get better' but how can it? Harry was my soul mate, my life and my best friend. I knew I would feel more pain from the minute he was physically removed from me; dead or alive, it felt like Harry was still with me right up to the day of the funeral.

I do believe in life after death and that's partly the reason why I will always feel that Harry is still 'with me', in spirit if not in body. I wanted the funeral not to be a public event but more about 'showing' Harry how much he had impacted on people's lives and how much 'ordinary' people loved him as a person. The service was held at St Edburgha's Church in Yardley, Birmingham. Some people had travelled hundreds of miles to be there; celebrities such as Duncan Bannatyne, Ben Shephard and Joe McElderry came to pay their respects; hundreds of local people lined the streets along the route of the funeral procession en route to the church and some people had decided to follow Harry's SpongeBob Square Pants coffin all the way to the church by foot. The thing that touched us the most was the attendance of some of Harry's beloved Twitter 'family' who had never met Harry before but somehow, Harry had made an impact on their lives.

The police even stopped the traffic along a very busy main road, the A45 Coventry Road, just for Harry, until the whole entourage had passed. I had a little smile to myself because we were still learning every day just how much people thought of Harry. We honestly never really expected any of it. Although we anticipated a full church, we never imagined that hundreds and hundreds of people would be lining the streets clapping, as the cars passed by. Even when we passed through a local shopping area, 'The Yew Tree', all the shoppers just stopped what they were doing and clapped as Harry's coffin passed by. Again, it hit home just how much Harry had impacted on everyone. I still didn't understand how an average eleven-year-old boy could receive such wonderful adulation. All of that because the last two years of his life had affected so many people that they had to pay their respects to our boy. Harry would have been so, so proud if he had known, when he was alive, how much he had touched people's lives, but he just didn't realise it himself. It was amazing that so many people wanted to honour him and support him on 'his' day. Maybe if he had known how popular he was, it may have changed him, but we will never know that. Knowing Harry, he wouldn't have changed one bit, however famous he became, though.

We insisted that all the pallbearers wore 'Harry bracelets' as they slowly carried his SpongeBob decorated coffin into the church for the service. The Reverend John Tsipouras said it was a day of sunshine and showers,

'The showers are the tears of loss of someone special to us, but we have sunshine to remember Harry's remarkable life.' That just about summed it up, really. Harry's sister Danielle read the congregation a moving poem about her brother, and X Factor winner Joe McElderry performed one of Harry's favourite karaoke songs, *The Climb*. Every time I heard Harry sing that song he really moved me and I couldn't believe Joe McElderry was singing it for us. You could see in his face the desperation to sing it well. The words to the song just really summed up Harry's life. Harry had always loved karaoke and most Friday nights, even during his illness, he would sleep for a couple of hours then wake up and come downstairs to belt out a few songs. *The Climb* was usually one of them, as the words to the song were just so fitting for Harry's 'journey', if you like. Harry definitely liked the song, which included the lyrics: 'I gotta be strong …just keep pushing on.' The song was so Harry. That's why I will always be eternally grateful that a star like Joe McElderry would offer to be at Harry's funeral and sing Harry's special song. For me, as Harry's mum, it gave me the sense of feeling that I knew I couldn't have given Harry a better send off than it turned out to be.

The mediaeval church was so full that many listened to the service on loudspeakers in the grounds and in the surrounding streets. Many of the congregation wore the colourful bracelets he had made while others wore T-shirts printed with a picture of Harry. I remember being totally oblivious to all the people in the church and, to this day, I couldn't tell you who was there or wasn't there, who I spoke to or how many people attended the service. I was just staring at Harry's coffin and watching the beautiful slideshow of happy, cheeky photos of Harry, remembering the good times I'd had with him. I was in a state of disbelief and my mind was a total blank. Throughout the service I just kept thinking: 'Today's about Harry and I have to do him proud.' There was no way I could crumble in front of all these people and I'm still the mother of Dani and Louie, who needed me to be OK. That's always been my outlook as a mother: life's not about me or my true feelings. My life's about my children and often we have to put our feelings aside for the sake of the children.

I managed to get up and do my reading and I genuinely don't know how I got through it. I just remember feeling so alone and empty inside, even though there were hundreds of people inside the church, and even more outside, listening to my every word. It was always Harry who got up to deliver speeches to (sometimes) hundreds of people but for me, it was the first time I'd had to do anything like that. But I did it, for Harry. It wasn't about me and I guess that's what got me through it.

It was only after the coffin was hidden by the curtains, towards the end of the funeral service, and we had arrived home after that horrendous day, that it struck us that we wouldn't ever see our Harry again. After such a rollercoaster ride over the previous four years, caring and attending to Harry's every need around the clock, we realised that Harry was no longer with us. That was it! Harry had been with me twenty-four hours a day. Wherever I was, Harry was with me. The reality of it all was now all too obvious for the first time since his passing. It felt like there was no tomorrow; for me there will be never be a tomorrow without Harry in my life, but, as they say, 'life has to go on'. Yes, life may have to go on, but I think that when you lose a child, whatever the reason, your life becomes about 'existence'. You seem to lose all sense of living, desire, ambition and dreams. You still have to get on with whatever's thrown at you, but now, after losing Harry, my life is about just getting through it, for sure. Normality and routine has to be found for Harry's amazing brother and sister, who have been through more in their childhood that most adults will ever encounter in a lifetime. Sadly for them, they – like Harry's dad and me – will always feel the pain of losing Harry. I wish they had been younger than they were when Harry died, as they have had the worst four years during such an impressionable time in their lives. As teenagers, they will never forget the pain and they have felt at such a loss and that breaks my heart as their mum. My life is now devoted to my three children and although Harry's gone now, I will always be his mum and aim to keep his dreams alive and I will always be there for Dani and Louie, every step of the way through their lives.

We all loved Harry very, very much – he was our special little boy; a 'normal' little boy really, but as a family we just thought: 'What now? What do we do now? Do we carry on Harry's campaign or close it down for good?' Harry had put the last two years of his life into his campaign. I had also put the last two years of my life into helping Harry and I just didn't know what to do at that point in time, as the pain was so raw. Somehow, Harry had this amazing quality of reaching out and touching people's hearts without really knowing it and that's a real God-given gift, but we didn't really appreciate that while he was with us. I had to stop and think how an eleven-year-old boy could have made such an impact on the lives of so many people he didn't even know. Some people are born with a certain gift, be it the natural ability to play football, to draw or paint, to sing or act, but Harry must have been born with the gift of helping others and making people happy. Harry was born to 'make it happen'.

Just after Harry passed away, I received a letter which just about summed up the impact his life (and his untimely death) had on people from all over the world. The letter was from a lady who worked in a care home and she followed Harry on Twitter and carried on following my 'Tweets' updating everyone about Harry's surgery. She wrote that she was working in the care home and sobbed her heart out when she read my Tweet that Harry had sadly passed away. Like most of his 'Twitfam' she didn't know Harry and just followed him because he somehow reached out and touched her life for that brief time he was alive. As a care worker, she attended to a ninety-year-old lady who had cancer and had always been very bitter because of it, so much so that she fell out with her family and that left her very much alone in the care home. After hearing about Harry's death, the care worker went to tell the old lady all about Harry's eventful life and how he had touched her own life and described all that he had achieved in a short space of time. Apparently, after being told about Harry, the old lady felt so ashamed of herself (for being so bitter) that she completely changed her outlook on life over the subsequent weeks. She also got back in touch with her daughter and started to go out shopping with her, something she apparently hadn't done for quite some time and she eventually became a nice person to be with again. All this was because of the impact Harry had on the care worker and, subsequently, on the old lady, just from hearing about his amazing story. It was lovely to receive that letter but generally, we hardly ever heard about the impact Harry had on people in such detail until his death. How he did that, I just don't know. He didn't have a 'plan' to be like that. It was just Harry being himself – a beautiful person.

I don't know if he had had a premonition or something, but it was as though he will always be around. Although we can't see him or touch him, his legacy will remain with us forever and that's the real harsh part of our family life moving forward.

7

Life After Harry – Making Harry's Dreams Happen

'Hopefully, Harry's legacy will live on forever.'
Ian Taylor (ex-footballer and an Ambassador for HHHO)

Harry definitely made things happen. I don't know how and I don't know why. I just know he did it in his own way. It is such a waste that he is no longer here to make any of his dreams happen. Quite frankly, I didn't understand it then, I don't get it now and I don't think I ever will comprehend why he's not here by my side today. It's one of those things I don't think anyone will ever understand; why people so young, or anybody for that matter, are lost to this horrible disease that we have no control over. That's why Harry was so intent on raising so much money to find a cure.

During those first few weeks after the funeral, my feelings were very raw; I think they will always be raw and life won't be the same again and, like I've said before, for me life is now all about 'existence' and making sure my family are safe and happy. I can't imagine me being the person I once was when Harry was alive. I look at the pictures of myself with Harry before he died and every one of them showed a sparkle in my eye and a truly happy face. I did take a good look at myself and, yes, I could have given up on life. After you lose a child, it's like your whole life has been ripped apart. Harry and I were such good mates as well as mother and son and that bond was so close, it was almost indescribable. I used to tell him all the time that he was my best friend, my hero and my inspiration. He was my little soul mate because I loved every second I spent with him. He brought so much humour, so much emotion and so much fun to my life. At first, I just wanted to crumble and hide away alone, but I couldn't do that because I needed to look after two other amazing children who had been through a lot over the previous four years or more, watching their brother go through hell. How selfish would it have been of me, as their mum, to have just given up? But inside, I felt like I wanted to just sit at home and grieve and pine for Harry just like any other mother probably would have. And who would have blamed anyone for doing that?

It would have been easy for me to put 'closure' to Harry's campaign, but it was as though something snapped inside of me one day and I thought: 'Why shouldn't I keep his dreams alive?' I needed to put aside the way I really felt and to carry on for the sake on my family. Harry's work was so important to him, but he's no longer around to carry on his dreams he started, but Harry taught me a lot; so much so that it would have felt like I would be letting Harry down if I didn't carry on progressing his dreams and continuing all that he stood for and 'making it happen' – for Harry.

If Harry was still alive now, I know he would have still been working tirelessly on his campaign. Even when he was in hospital and knew he was about to undergo major brain surgery, the only things he could think about were other people and his campaign. I remember one day he was supposed to deliver a speech at a dinner for children with cancer, but he had to be rushed into hospital. Harry was devastated to have let them down, and he insisted on writing the speech for them, so that someone else could read it out on his behalf, as he couldn't be there to deliver it himself. As a result, Harry received loads of toys which he then subsequently arranged to go to the Neurosurgical and Cancer wards at Birmingham Children's Hospital. The toys came from Diane at 'Be Cancer Aware' and it was Diane who Harry was supposed to deliver his speech to. That was the kind of boy Harry was, always so selfless and those acts of kindness made me even more determined to carry on with all of his work. Harry had created all the tools and maybe I was meant to carry on as Harry's 'messenger', putting all his plans into place and rolling out his dreams. For me, I never want any parent to feel the pain I went through – and will always feel – and for that reason Harry's work had to continue. There just has to be some way of finding a cure for brain cancer.

Darren, as Harry's father, also suffered the same emotions of hurt, anger, frustration and disbelief which I think we will all feel for the rest of our lives. For me and my family, that shining light has gone out and it's like we have disappeared into a 'lost world' which is dark and dismal, just like being down a big black hole where there's no escape. It is a place where I don't think either Darren or I will ever come out of. People say 'time is a healer' but having had a child like Harry in our lives – and then losing him so suddenly and tragically after only eleven short years – I don't think we, as a family, will ever recover and we won't be the same family again, that's for sure. Looking back at all the photos of us together, with Harry in them all, you can see the closeness and happiness we once had. Whatever problems we faced, nothing was more important than coming together as a family. Whatever was going on behind the scenes, we were a picture of sheer joy and happiness, because our bond and love for each other as a family was greater than anything else you can imagine. Like everyone else, we had a lot of stress and bad times along the way, but looking back, I didn't realise just how close we were as a family unit. I always knew, during the times I spent with Harry, that he and I had a special mother and son bond and I very often just think of his name and I want to give him a big hug, but he's no longer there and I feel an emptiness that is totally impossible to express properly. All this changed us as a family so quickly and, deep down, I know the harsh reality is that we have to get on with our lives, as there are two other beautiful children we have to bring up and develop into adults. Harry's loss has left such a hole in our lives, but his short but eventful life has made a massive impact and I hope Danielle and Louie can learn from these experiences and excel in their adult lives. I can't imagine what they went through, as children and as Harry's brother and sister, because they had very different emotions to my own. All I can do now is to be there for them, just as I was with Harry. I've never had a brother or sister, so I can't ever really know what they are feeling. Only they can. I can only tell you that I hurt immensely for them, too.

Dani and Louie were both very close to Harry and we brought them up to be that close so, for them, it's closure to four years of hell, watching their brother go through all that suffering. Not only that, they suffered as well, as it affected their lives at home and at school. During the time that Harry was ill, my life was dominated by looking after Harry and making sure he was where he was meant to be, whether that was at the hospital, school or at some function. Don't forget: I was his 'bag carrier and chauffeur'. We always tried our hardest to give Dani and Louie their own time, but it all had a massive impact on them, too. Every time Harry was admitted to hospital, they didn't have a mum at home and their dad had to become a combined mum and dad, as I was always at Harry's bedside. They both know that I love them all equally and, God forbid, if it was either of them who had been ill, I would have done exactly the same. Sometimes in life you try to catch up for the time you lose with your loved ones, but it's not always possible. So for them now, I hope this closure is a turning point in their lives, where they can now have an 'easier' adult life and that they continue to grow up into very beautiful people, which they already are. I know they will and I am already very proud of everything they have done and will do in their lives. The three of my children are wonderful, beautiful people who just deserve everything the world has to offer. I hope that it's their time now for things to fall into place and for them to have a smooth adult life, but at the same time, they should never forget the time they spent with Harry and what they went through with their little brother. I'm sure the whole 'journey' will have made them stronger and it will ensure that, as adults, they retain the important qualities in life of a true understanding of what really matters most …each other.

Ever since Danielle and Louie lost their brother in October 2011, they have obviously found it hard to cope with everyday life and it does take time for people to learn to live with their loss, but for Danielle, she was approaching a crucial time in her life and she went straight back into doing her A Levels, even though she probably wasn't as switched on as she was before Harry's death and she still gets very emotional and gets uptight and tearful from time to time, thinking about her little brother. Louie excelled at school after losing his brother, which I found hard to understand, but I guess, because Louie found it hard to let his emotions out, it was his way of coping with it all. Danielle is very much like me in that way; unlike Louie, she will let out her feelings very easily. Either way, I am so proud of them and how they have coped and adapted to life without their little brother. Given the circumstances, I know we made it as good as it could possibly have been and I just hope that, if there is a God, Harry's up there now as an angel, watching over them, keeping them safe, happy and guiding them.

For the first six months none of us liked being at home and we couldn't sit and relax. Sunday roast dinners seem a thing of the past as well, as we used to all sit together and it will never be 'right' without that fifth chair. The loss of Harry was immense at the time (and always will be) but we will all try our best to get on because we simply have to. Inside, I think I will grieve for the rest of my life for losing Harry. Without my little mate, the world seems a very dark and lonely place. Of course, if he had lived he would have grown up like his brother and sister and become more independent, but to have a child by your side 24/7 and then have him suddenly snatched away means every single day is 'different' for me now and whatever I'm doing, it's alone, and that hurts like hell.

At first I wasn't sure of the way forward, either for myself, my family or for Harry's campaign. I honestly imagined that would be it. Harry was gone now and I assumed that the no one would be interested in the campaign without him, but soon after Harry had passed away, so many people started to contact me and many just wanted to show their support to keep his memory alive and do their bit to continue the cause. I was inundated with emails and messages from children who wanted to do good because they'd been inspired by Harry. Not just here in the UK but globally. To me, it identified a need that children really wanted something like Harry had created, to guide them to do good things. It was partly due to the response from the children that I just had to keep this going for them, for Harry and for the families going through the same battle with brain cancer that we had just encountered. I know it will happen for a long

Harry in his beloved paddling pool.

Karaoke Harry

Harry and the CEO of Virgin Media.

Harry spreading love at Virgin Media offices.

With his friend Duncan Bannatyne at a Skydiving event.

Travelling in style to London, June 2011.

There's one for everyone – Harry's colourful bracelets.

Just a small collection of beads.

Harley House' plaque – made by Harry.

Inside 'Harley House'.

With Duncan's book on a train to Darlington, June 2011.

Robert Harley

The two of us at Hamleys in London.

Selling bracelets outside Asda.

Simply Harry.

Sir Cliff Richard wearing 'Harry bracelets'.

Spreading 'Harry love' on the radio.

Just the start of it.

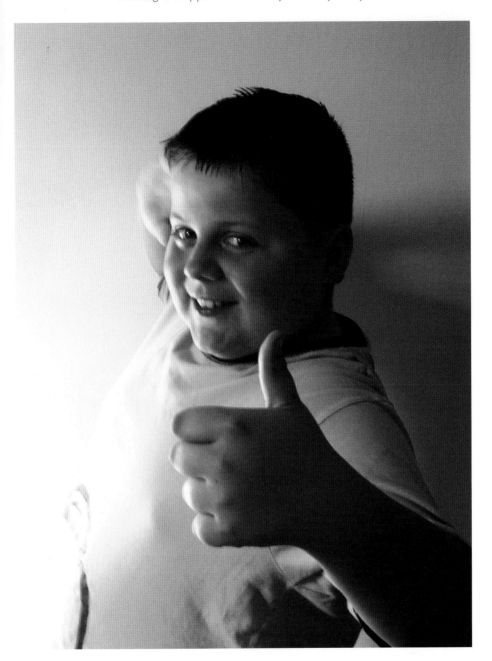

Harry always had a positive and cheery outlook.

Harry with Jools Tait, Frank Lampard and John Terry.

A montage of pictures taken in London July 26th 2012 prior to the Olympic Torch procession.

Harry and I at his launch.

Harry with his good friend Tom Ross at BRMB (Now Free Radio).

Harry before his first treatment, April 2007.

Our family jigsaw – the five of us.

Promoting the Npower health through warmth scheme.

Harry with Gary Linekar and Ben Shephard at the HHHO launch, May 2011.

Harry and Chris Evans at the Children's Champions Award in London, March 2010.

ITV followed Harry to Number 10 Downing Street, October 2009.

Harry's celebrity friends.

time to come, but I never want any parent to feel the pain we feel after losing Harry. We soon realised that Harry had started something which just couldn't end – a legacy potentially so large that we just couldn't close it all down. Giving up would be like giving up on him and I would never ever do that.

After a few months pondering which direction we should take, it was down to the great British public (and beyond) that we decided that Harry's dreams must live on - 'the show must go on' we thought. After all, he started it to help others. Harry would have been so disappointed watching us from 'on high' if we just 'shut up shop' and let his dreams disappear. And the only person who could carry on his legacy was me. It would have been so easy to put closure to this chapter in our lives, but, as I've said, I just didn't feel it was the right thing to do as it would be like giving up on Harry. Everything I had done for the campaign was for Harry and I couldn't give up on his dreams and ideas just because Harry wasn't here anymore. Rather than Harry making all the decisions, I could have ultimate control of the campaign and the direction it would take and it would be in keeping with Harry's philosophy. I wouldn't want anyone to go through what Harry went through and what we went through as a family, so that way of thinking made it easier to make the decision to carry on the 'HelpHarryHelpOthers' campaign, albeit without the most important person at the helm: the 'boss', Harry. Giving up on 'HelpHarryHelpOthers' wasn't an option for me, no matter how I felt. He made his campaign his life and I had to keep it alive.

I remember there was a young girl called Tilly whom we met at the hospital just before Harry went into surgery and Harry was heartbroken for her. One day in hospital, just after her brain surgery and while Harry was awaiting his, Harry went to the toilet on the ward and walked past the HDU section where Tilly was staying for a few days after her surgery. When he came back to his bed he was so tearful and said to me: 'That's why I do what I do, mum. One day there will be a cure.' To Harry it was about the awareness that he wanted to get across to people rather than it being for personal gain. If he had the opportunity to speak in front of fifty or five hundred people he would do it, because he was making those people aware of his campaign. I think that's what people saw in Harry and how he touched so many lives; just his selfless nature. I remember whenever Harry was being interviewed and they asked him: 'What are your hopes for your campaign?' The answer back from Harry would always be the same: 'I just want it to be massive.' His focus and passion was about finding a cure for brain cancer.

Harry had great vision and had a number of dreams and goals he wanted to fulfil. Funnily enough, one was to write a book about his life. However, his ultimate dream was to find a cure for brain cancer so that nobody else would go through what he had. Another dream was that he wanted to meet all of his 'Twitfam' (even though there were over 98,000 of them when Harry was alive). He loved Twitter, after Ben Shephard had encouraged him to use it. He loved his followers and he wanted to create an event so that it gave everyone an opportunity to meet him. He dreamt up an event which would have seen him travel in a classic car (like one of Robert's) from John O'Groats to Land's End, stopping off at certain strategic places. He wanted to call it 'Harry Tours the UK for Robert'. He wanted it to be a national campaign. It was his way of giving something back to his followers and thanking them for their support and generosity.

One of Harry's ultimate goals was for 'HelpHarryHelpOthers' to be as recognised as 'Race for Life'. He was so determined to increase the profile of his campaign and, as he kept saying, 'spread Harry Love' wherever he had the opportunity. He was so determined to 'make it happen' and knew that it would only become such a huge campaign with hard work and lots of determination, yet to Harry it wasn't hard work. It was in his nature to be kind and to help others and for him, every minute was pure fun, no matter what he was doing and whoever he was meeting.

As Ben Shephard once quoted when talking about Harry in an interview: 'Nothing was too big for Harry. Nothing was too small for Harry.' That, in my eyes, made Harry very special. Quite often, as charitable stories grow into big concerns, I have seen them sometimes become too 'corporate' and lose that personal touch and 'from the heart' passion. Harry would never have let that happen to his own campaign if he'd still been around and I sure as hell won't as I continue with all of Harry's work. Harry always said that if the day came when it wasn't about him, Robert and all the people out there suffering with brain cancer, he would refuse to continue his campaign and that's the philosophy every charity should adopt and one I decided I would continue. Harry busted a gut to do all his own events and he wanted his 'brand' to be big enough to be recognised and his name to be included in all of his events.

'HelpHarryHelpOthers' was always going to be a unique campaign and when I look at some of the charities and campaigns around and look at all the celebrities out there backing them, I just think there was no campaign like Harry's and there was no one person quite like Harry.

As I've mentioned before, there are lots of campaigns which have been started by parents in memory of someone who sadly passed away, but this charity is very different to all of those because this was Harry's creation not mine and Harry started the campaign when he was very much alive. He made it what it is today using all his own tools. I just simply wanted to continue the work he had started. Even after the few months following his death, I definitely see myself as Harry's messenger now. He's still the boss from Heaven. None of the dreams or ideas were down to me – they were all down to one little boy called Harry Moseley.

One of the first decisions I had to make was whether to keep Harry's Twitter account open (@harry_moseley) and I just had to keep all of his 'Twitfam' informed of what was going on, so that was an easy decision. It is very important to me to keep everything personal to what Harry stood for and that included his beloved 'Twitfam'. All the messages that I received via Twitter saying that I'm 'amazing' – well, I'm not 'amazing' because I'm just using Harry's tools and ideas and just rolling out what he started and what he would have done anyway, if he had still been here. My aim is what Harry's aim was: that the campaign will get bigger and bigger and eventually we will help to find a cure for brain cancer, along with all the other amazing brain tumour charities.

There was no real plan as such, just a number of ideas and dreams Harry had, a 'Wish List' if you like. But soon after letting everyone know that the campaign was 'business as usual', literally hundreds of people I didn't even know contacted me asking if they could organise events to raise money for Harry's charity. There was anything from 'Skydiving For Harry', 'Walk For Harry', 'Cycling For Harry' and even 'Pub Crawl For Harry'. You name it, I had people contact me about it. Up and down the country (and indeed all around the world), people had begun to organise events to raise money in the name of Harry. Right up to the time Harry went into hospital for his second operation, he had attended all of his eighty events, but it was such a shame he wouldn't be here to witness all of these events in honour of his memory. They had all been organised by people I didn't even know and even Harry didn't know, apart from their connection to Twitter.

Some months before Harry died, he was interviewed on his favourite radio station, BRMB radio in Birmingham (now Free Radio) by Tom Ross, and he talked about his tumour and his campaign. Tom asked him questions like: 'How much do you want to raise?' and 'Where do you want to take the campaign?' Harry's response was the usual one to that question: 'I just want to make it massive.' By that, Harry meant he wanted his 'brand' to be recognised just as Cancer Research UK was recognised nationwide. He didn't necessarily want to be the biggest or the best charity, but he just wanted his brand to be recognised everywhere. Most charities, if not all charities out there have the same objective and that is to find a cure for whatever they stand for and Harry's charity was and is no different; to find a cure for brain cancer. It was what drove him to do so many events himself. After that interview with Tom Ross, Harry said to me: 'Mum, I've just got to write off to BRMB. I want the Walkathon next year (2012) to be for my campaign, so we can help people in Birmingham.' Unfortunately, Harry didn't get a chance to write that letter, but his dream amazingly came alive shortly after his death because BRMB announced early in 2012 that the Walkathon was to be renamed 'Walk For Harry' for that year, in memory of, and as a tribute to Harry. The Walkathon is an annual event which encompasses a twenty-six mile circuit around one of Birmingham's circular bus routes and it has been taking place for over twenty-five years. The walk was one of the largest charity events in Birmingham. Yes, it was very soon after his passing, but it was one of Harry's biggest dreams and my life now is about ticking off all of Harry's dreams as they are each put into place. I thought to myself: 'Why shouldn't it happen just because Harry's not here anymore?' – and it did.

Therefore, as soon as the announcement was made, there was never any doubt where the funds were going to be donated to. We decided that the funds raised from the Walkathon 2012 would go towards the two charities intimately connected to Harry. One was to support the brain tumour research project being led at Birmingham Children's Hospital by Harry's consultant, Dr Andrew Peet. The other project was the refurbishment of The Acorns Hospice at Selly Oak, Birmingham where we were all looked after so well. All funds raised were to be split equally between the two charities.

Birmingham Children's Hospital look after children all over the UK for all sorts of illnesses. Dr Peet, Dr Kirk and their teams had taken great care looking after Harry for the hardest four years of our lives. Harry always tried to support his consultant and this would be our way of saying 'thank you' to him. We will always support his amazing work for all those people up and down the country who are fighting brain cancer.

I had heard about Acorns before contacting them after Harry had passed away, but I never had an insight into what they did and how wonderful they were. Acorns is a registered charity offering a network of care for life-limited and life-threatened children and young people and their families, across three hospices in the heart of England. These children and young people don't expect to reach adulthood and require specialist care twenty-four hours a day, seven days a week and they currently support over 600 children and 865 families, including those who are bereaved. Acorns is the only organisation that provides this level of care to these vulnerable youngsters whilst offering a range of support services to the whole family to help them cope at every stage of their child's life and beyond into bereavement. Acorns said to me that during 2011, they had the highest number of children with brain cancer passing through their care than they have ever had. Incidentally, two weeks before Harry died, we were in the process of arranging for Harry to go there on a weekly basis to take baths and showers, as our home wasn't suitable for Harry. If we had managed to bring him home to care for him, this would only have been possible because of Acorns. However, they have special private rooms where families can spend time with their loved one just before they are laid to rest, so when Harry did pass away, we were allowed to take Harry's body to Acorns so we could spend the last days with him in his 'special' SpongeBob bedroom and say 'goodbye' to him. We treasure those moments we had with Harry at Acorns and I was so grateful to them for allowing us that time.

Ultimately, the money raised from the 'Walk for Harry' event will be going towards helping families who have been going through what we have been through with Harry. I specifically wanted (and Harry wanted) his 'God', Dr Peet, to benefit so it could help fund his brain cancer research projects. When Harry passed away, he had helped raise over £650,000 and some of that helped Dr Peet's projects and in fact fully funded them for three years.

Some time ago, Harry wrote down a number of his dreams on his 'Wish List' and as soon as I had it confirmed by BRMB that the Walkathon was to be in memory of Harry, I saw Harry's list in my memory and I ticked off Harry's first dream – BRMB Walkathon. Check. 'I've done that, H. What's next?' Life is so different now without Harry and it is all about balancing the way we dedicate time to our other two children, Danielle and Louie, and still make Harry's dreams come true. Those are my aspirations now and it all started with the Walkathon.

Harry's philosophy was always to please everyone else and he always thought ahead when he was making his bracelets. Harry had bought a garden shed (which he named 'Harley House') and sometimes he would sit there all day long, making his bracelets and fulfilling his orders. The shed was kitted out with a table and it was full of boxes of coloured beads and elastic bands. It was a real one man production line, although the family and friends were often asked to help out on occasions when the order books were filling up. The idea of making bracelets was so simple that the skills are transferable to anyone. With that in mind, a perfect idea was to roll out this simple task, starting in our local area by opening a 'Harry Shop' where children (and adults) could come along, free of charge, not just to learn how to make bracelets, but to make use of their talents and to release their passion about life and the things they care about and are interested in doing. The aim for me was to help children figure out what they want out of life and also how they can be good and do good things and how they can help others, which was what Harry believed in. Harry loved giving his speeches to schools and talking to the children about his ideas and he loved seeing the children get involved in making bracelets and being interested in his philosophy of helping others. I saw this as an extension of that and it's definitely an opportunity for children of all ages to get involved, which is the most important thing. When things in this world make our children sad, we should encourage them to use all their energy and help them realise their potential, because only they can do something about it. Harry's workshops will help them put together a tailored plan (based on their individual skills and personalities) to go and make a difference, whatever they are passionate about. With this in mind, we will be running Harry's #Selfless Saturdays from Harry's charity headquarters to engage children and adults in the community in the first instance. Using Harry's tools we plan to run free workshops for children and, once we have identified their individual skills and established what each child really cares about, we are going to help them with all the tools Harry created and put together their own fundraising plan for whatever they care about. Harry was a very 'special' kid, but all children are special and we want them to also realise they can achieve anything they put their head and their heart into.

Of course, opening a charity shop involves immense time, effort and money, but this could only have been done if I made changes to Harry's campaign as it was, because it had always been linked to other charities. Harry always wanted his own registered charity called 'HelpHarryHelpOthers' but I always feared Harry might take a backward step in his health at some stage. Obviously, it would be a huge commitment to undertake, not only to set it up as an official Registered Charity but to continue with it and I honestly think that was the way to go because it would be structured and be fully in our control and we would tailor it to everything that Harry stood for. Apart from the registered charity in Harry's name, we have created the 'Harry Moseley SMILE Fund' which aims to help families going through the same 'journey' by creating 'smiles' at Christmas or birthdays, providing short breaks away or simply helping with household items if families are experiencing financial hardship. Finally we also set up the 'Robert Harley Fund' which will help fund services (such as hospices, hospital wards, community nurses etc. who specifically support end of life and palliative care) that look after those people like Harry and Robert who, sadly, can't be saved.

Now that our other two children are older and very independent and making their own way in life, this gives me something to focus on. Setting up and registering Harry's own charity was like ticking off another thing on Harry's 'Wish List'. I just think: what better job could I ever have than running Harry's own charity, named after Harry and putting my heart and soul into something which meant so much to him and something we always worked on together? Harry did so much good work but he never saw what he did – his campaign – as 'work' as such, but as 'something he just did'. He loved every minute of it, whatever he was doing to help others. There were lots of times I remember saying to Harry: 'Don't you ever get fed up, don't you ever want to stop?' He always replied: 'No, mum. I love it. I'm helping others and I have the best feeling inside me.' Speaking from the heart, I honestly think that I can never ever move on from losing Harry and I don't ever want to, as he and my other two children have always been the most important people in my life; they simply are my life. Not continuing 'HelpHarryHelpOthers' and returning to a 'normal' full-time job (like the one I used to do before Harry became too ill) would have been like moving on from Harry and rebuilding my life and that's simply something I never wanted to do. If Harry's looking down on me – and I truly believe he is – all I want him to see is that we are still the best team and that every day for the rest of my life he will be a huge part of it.

Another part of his campaign which was close to Harry's heart was the 'schools initiative', which will soon be rolled out across the country. Harry made quite a few contacts with schools (some of which he visited to deliver his speech) up and down the UK and since Harry's death, we have been inundated with further enquiries from schools, not just in the UK, asking me to come and deliver Harry's speech to their pupils. I even had emails from as far away as Australia and Dubai, from people who have followed Harry or have heard about Harry's work and they really wanted to spread the word. Harry hadn't realised what a special and unique campaign he had created in rolling out the 'school's initiative'. Obviously, it won't be Harry delivering his own speech in the future, but now it can be taken one step further and maybe it could be a confident school kid who feels empowered to deliver the speech to his fellow pupils during an assembly, for example. After all, there's always a 'Harry' in every school; that confident, cheeky lad who has a lot to say and even more to give. It was always Harry's dream to roll out this initiative across the country, but there was only one Harry, so he loved to go into the schools himself to talk to the children. The idea of empowering children to do good things like Harry is so appealing to me. The speech would be all the same words Harry used and the same ideas will be delivered.

The basic idea of the initiative could include someone delivering the speech; a few people could make the bracelets; someone else could be responsible for the accounting and another team would be in charge of sales. Not only does it help children understand the basics of business (including profit, loss, marketing, finance, IT, speaking skills etc.) but this project will give children a greater understanding of all elements of business very early on in their lives. Then there's the communication in newsletters and school assemblies and maybe they could go outside into the local community, making people aware that the bracelets are for sale and spreading the news about the project. I think that will get a lot of children thinking about what the money they make can go towards. Not only will the children get to learn valuable skills, but they will raise money for charity and also for their own school fund, too. It will get them thinking that 'if Harry can do it, then there is no reason why anyone else can't do what Harry did', but sometimes children need that extra encouragement and empowerment to give them the self-belief to start something.

I really see the 'schools initiative' being run along the lines of The Apprentice or Dragons Den type themes, so I can't see anyone other than Duncan Bannatyne being the 'face' of the campaign. I think he would be an excellent role model for children to follow. Duncan sometimes gets some unfair press and I think it would be great for him to launch this initiative. Duncan isn't just a celebrity who has come out of nowhere. He has grafted all his life, built up his empire from nothing and made his millions. I don't think people actually realise what Duncan has actually done in giving to a lot of charities, not just Pilgrims and 'HelpHarryHelpOthers'. When Harry came home from hospital for a week when he was really ill, Duncan kindly offered to put me and my family up at one of his hotels for a few days for a break; no one was aware of that at the time. Unfortunately, because of Harry's declining condition, we had to get in touch with Duncan to say that we couldn't make it on that occasion, although it was a lovely gesture. I had to be no more than half an hour away from Birmingham Children's Hospital in case we had to rush Harry back into hospital, which is exactly what happened. Duncan does a lot more than most people are aware of and more than he is given credit for. I would imagine that's true of a lot of celebrities. As it happened, Duncan made a very large donation to Harry's charity when Harry died and credit to him for that – he didn't have to do it. So, all in all, I'm full of absolute admiration for Duncan, especially for being Harry's friend and that's also the reason we asked him to be an Ambassador for the 'HelpHarryHelpOthers' registered charity.

Already, at the time of writing this book in the summer of 2012, things are falling into place for Harry's dreams and the team of trustees and ambassadors we chose were all very special and personal to Harry while he was alive. They were all friends to Harry or have subsequently become friends of mine. They were originally inspired by Harry when he was alive and were also there at the end of his life. If I wasn't able to roll out Harry's work and keep it personal to all that Harry stood for, I wouldn't do it at all. It's all about teamwork and Harry now has a superb team behind him.

One of the 'team' of Ambassadors is the footballer, John Terry. John was so inspired by Harry's story that a few months after they met Harry at an England Footballers Federation event, Harry invited John to his official launch of his campaign in London. Unfortunately, John was unable to attend as he had a meeting elsewhere. The meeting which prevented John attending the official launch was to do with nominating Harry to be a torchbearer for the 2012 London Olympics. Although Harry wasn't here to be a torchbearer, a couple of months after Harry's passing we were informed that even though the Olympic officials knew of Harry's death, they still wanted to offer the place as he had been specifically selected and so they asked me if I would like to carry it in Harry's memory. All of that was thanks to John Terry. I, of course, accepted and while I knew it would be a really emotional day because Harry (who would have been just twelve years old and one of the youngest torchbearers there) should have been there himself to carry his torch. I had to do this for Harry because, if I didn't take his place it would have gone to someone else and Harry still deserved to have his moment. Harry would have been so touched by John's gesture and he truly deserved it so I carried the torch round the Chelsea football ground at Stamford Bridge in West London on 26th July 2012.

Amazingly, Harry's efforts are still being acknowledged and since his passing, he was commended and won a 'Lifetime Achievement Award' from JustGiving for all the money he raised through the use of their service. He's also won an 'Outstanding Achievement Award' from Cancer Research UK, not to forget a national award for 'Fundraiser of the Year 2012' by the Institute of Fundraising. Obviously for us it's extremely sad that Harry wasn't with us to accept those tremendous awards himself and as a family it was extremely hard to take in and it just seemed so very 'bittersweet'. However, all of his trophies mentioned, together with his 'Britain's Kindest Kid Award' and the 'Children's Champions Award' are where they belong, at home surrounding his SpongeBob ashes casket on the sideboard in our lounge. Harry was always a big part of our family and he will always be a big part of our home and it will always be the five of us, forever.

So now we continue with the next chapter for Harry and 'HelpHarryHelpOthers' and whilst Harry is not physically here he will always be a huge part of everyday for both us personally as a family and as his charity. It's something I simply have to do. As a family we have lived and breathed brain cancer for four long years and it robbed us of our precious boy. We know through our own experience where all people with brain cancer are being failed.

Our objectives have been based on areas we know need vast funding. Our main focus is to 'Help Cure' giving money direct to brain cancer research projects as its the least funded cancer and yet it now kills more children than any other cancer. 'Help Cope' (the 'Harry Moseley SMILE FUND') will, as its name says, provide 'smiles' for families going through cancer and help them cope that little bit more with taking away financial pressure at Christmas/birthdays or by providing household items that they cannot afford. Finally we have the 'Help Care' (the Robert Harley Fund) which will support the wonderful services of those that specifically look after terminally ill and end of life care.

I dedicate the rest of my life to this and for all those reading this book that are living in hope – WE WILL FIND THAT CURE.

As Harry was always humbled by the support he received, as a charity we are different and we want to thank everyone that supports us. How will we do this? by giving back to the children by empowering them to be good people and by using all the tools that Harry himself created. We will be running free workshops for children at Harry's 'Harley House' charity headquarters to help them make a difference to whatever cause is close to their hearts. Harry was a shining example of the fact that, regardless of age, wellbeing and lifestyle, kids really can achieve anything if they are passionate enough about something.

We will also be rolling our Harry's schools intiative nationally to inspire kids to get involved with charity whilst raising money for their school's own fund along with them learning all round basic business skills.

What Harry created was unique and his charity like his bracelets is 'hand made with love for all people with cancer'. 'HelpHarryHelpOthers' will always be about Harry and all those living in hope. This I promise.

Thank You

'You made it happen H, I hope you never forget that.'

Since Harry's death on 8th October 2011, there has been an amazing response from his followers, including many celebrities who organised events to raise money for Harry's chosen charities and to raise the profile of brain cancer awareness in the UK. There are too many people to mention all of them, but my family and I would like to thank the following people who have organised events up and down the UK and abroad. For everyone else who has held events and supported Harry's amazing work, I thank you from the bottom of my heart for believing in Harry, his work and his dreams. Harry may not be on earth anymore, but I hope you can support his dreams of helping others moving forwards.

Firstly, I would like to personally acknowledge **Simon Goodyear** for helping me achieve one of Harry's dreams in compiling and writing this biography from my thoughts and memories of my beautiful son. Hopefully the book will have an impact and remind everyone who reads it of what is truly important in life.

Secondly, here is a list of some of the fantastic groups and events:

Walk For Harry 2012
– The renamed Free Radio Walkathon

CyclingForHarry
– A group who cycled from Birmingham to Wembley Stadium for HHHO.

RunningForHarry
– A group of people wanting to raise money and awareness for HHHO.

150mileWalk4Harry
– A group of Aston Villa fans walking the 150 miles from Villa Park in Birmingham to Carrow Road, home of Norwich City.

Harry's Tube Runners
– Steven Whyley organised an event to run the 450 miles and 270 stations of the London Underground network with the aim of raising £10,000 for HHHO and Cancer Research UK.

Pub Crawl For Harry
– Enough said!

Hiking For Harry
– A number of hiking events were organised up and down the UK in memory of Harry.

AuthorsHelpingHarry
–A group of writers based in the USA came together to raise money for Harry.

FootballForHarry
– John Hanks organised a charity football match involving Aston Villa Old Stars.

Pete Ellis (www.harryscharityball.com)
– Peter Ellis has helped to fulfil another of Harry's dreams by organising the first annual Charity Ball in Harry's Memory which will be held at the ICC In Birmingham on 19th October 2012.

I would also like to personally thank the following people or organisations who have been part of Harry's life and will continue to be part of my life moving forward:

Harrys beloved 'Twitfam'
To all Harry's beloved 'Twitfam', who used to Tweet Harry often. You all tweeted fun, support and love for Harry. It was you all who really encouraged Harry to keep going and you had a massive impact on his determination to do more and more. I thank you all for believing in Harry and creating so much laughter and friendship for him. You stuck by him through his good days and bad and now you are all a huge part of my life as I continue with Harry's Twitter account. You will always be in Harry's heart for sure, as you are in mine.

Blakenhale School
The biggest part of Harry's life. His whole life was spent here and you all know I was very sad when he left at his prom. You helped me raise three amazing children and because of that, I will always hold a special place in my heart for you all.

Dr Peet and Dr Kirk and teams
Your tireless efforts in supporting all children, like Harry, with life-threatening illnesses are admirable. You are two amazing consultants who looked after Harry with such compassion and care and every young training doctor should aspire to be like you both. In my eyes, you have the 'whole package'. I will never forget your support for Harry and all of us as a family and we miss you dearly.

Kelly Nunn, Ellen and family
You have all supported Harry by helping make his special bracelets. I will never forget the help and support you gave during the four months in hospital with Harry, when you managed Harry's campaign for him. If it wasn't for you all, Harry's campaign would have stopped. You let me concentrate on what was important and I will always love you all.

Acorns Hospice
A huge 'thank you' to David Black and all at Acorns Children's Hospice who took such great care of my beautiful boy after his passing. Although he had passed away, you treated him with true compassion, care and dignity, which will always be remembered by us as a family.

Harry's Ambassadors
Duncan Bannatyne, John Terry, Ben Shephard, Oliver Phelps, James Phelps, Wincey Willis, Tom Ross, Ed James, Michael Johnson and Ian Taylor.

Thank you for allowing our 'normal' little boy into your lives and staying in touch with him after he inspired you. Your friendship was something Harry was very proud of and I will always be eternally grateful for the happy memories you gave us. I would also like to thank you for helping me to keep Harry's work and dreams alive and for believing in him, even though he's not with us anymore.

Harry's Trustees
Sarah Moss, Kelly Nunn and family, Trina Harley, Ed James, Tom Ross, Tim Andrews and Peter Ellis.

Thank you all for your friendships with Harry and thank you for supporting him while he was here. It's only because of you all wishing to support me that Harry's dream of becoming a Registered Charity becomes a reality and I can ensure that Harry's vision will always be at the forefront so we can continue to 'HelpHarryHelpOthers'.

Cancer Research UK
Thank you for believing in Harry and his campaign and for introducing him to some wonderful people. A special thank goes to the team who supported Harry, especially Davina Yanful. The work you do is amazing and although 'HelpHarryHelpOthers' is now a registered charity, I'm sure 'together we will beat cancer'.

Virgin Media plc

A huge thumbs-up for inviting Harry to your London and Birmingham offices. To the Board of Directors and all the staff involved, I thank you for giving your valuable time, sitting with Harry to give him advice. You will never know how much that day meant to Harry and I have Harry's special gifts from you in a special place along with 'RED'. Your support since Harry's passing is very much appreciated and I hope that we can stay in touch always. The Virgin Media visit was Harry's last visit and also the one he was most proud of. You have all given me some very special memories. For this, I thank you all.

Combute

Thank you to you both for designing and building Harry's very personal new website **www.hhho.co.uk** which accurately reflects 'my Harry'. It's bright, cheery and contains everything Harry created. You know Harry's charity just has to stay personal to Harry and will always be about him and I thank you, Rob and Lucy, from the bottom of my heart for capturing that on his wonderful website.

Joanna Gilbert

Joanna is a commercial artist from 'Your Branded Art':
www.yourbrandedart.com – and painted the picture which appears on the back cover/front cover of the special editions of this book. The painting is called 'I See' and it represents how Harry sees the good in everything; his outlook is pure and positive. A reference to the 'HelpHarryHelpOthers' Charity is on his sleeve as that is where he wears his heart. The coloured circles symbolise the beads he uses for bracelets and finally the Twitter bird perched on his shoulder represents his friends and fans, all 98,000 of them. Since you presented the painting to Harry, it has hung in our lounge and will continue to do so forever.

And I'm saving the best 'til last.

Danielle and Louie

A huge 'thank you' to my amazing children, Dani and Louie. Why? Because you were the best ever sister and brother that Harry could ever have wished for. I am so immensely proud of you both. You are beautiful people, both inside and out, and I hope life treats you very kindly moving forward, as you both deserve it. I love you both so, so much.

To Harry

In the space of just two and a half years you created an inspirational campaign which as you dreamed of is now your own registered charity called 'Help Harry Help Others'. You have inspired adults and children alike around all four corners of the globe with your positive outlook and the tools you created.

You selflessly organised and attend over 80 events for the sake of others going through your 'journey' and helped to raise a staggering £750,000 which has risen now to over £1.1 million (at the time of writing).

The world felt a huge loss when you fell asleep but no one more than your family. You have my word that you will always be remembered like you wanted, but not as 'Harry the boy the with brain tumour', but as 'Harry the boy who helped people with brain tumours'.

Quite simply, 'thank you' for being my son, my best friend and my hero. I loved every minute of every day with you. You filled my life with joy and laughter and the best memories I could ever wish for. I loved the short time we shared and I cannot wait to be with you again one day. You will always be a huge part of my life.

Sleep tight, my angel, until we meet again.

God Bless.

Mom. xxxx